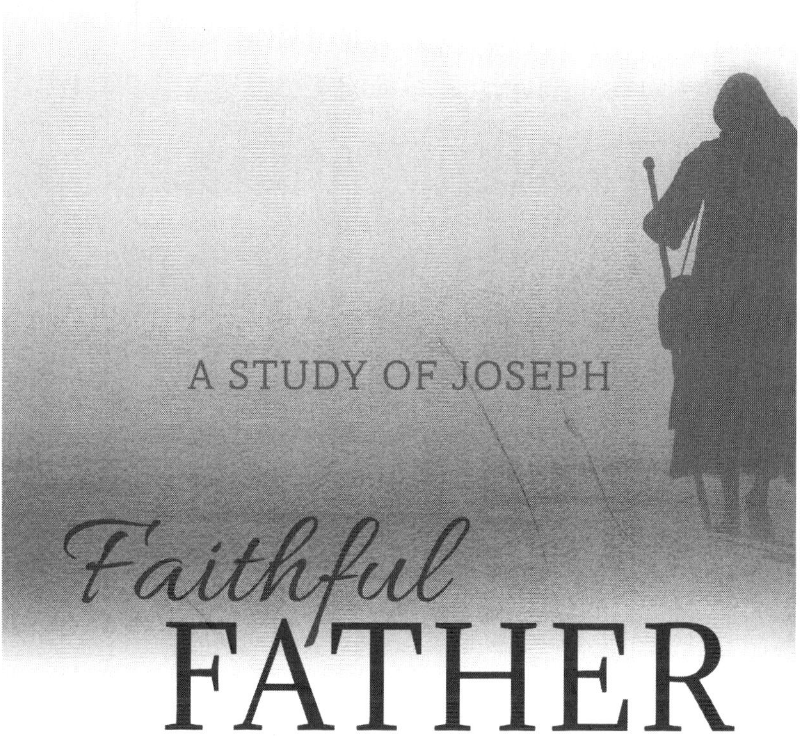

A STUDY OF JOSEPH

Faithful FATHER

WAYNE BRAUDRICK
and JEREMY MIKESKA

STONE TOWER PRESS

Faithful Father: A Study of Joseph

Stone Tower Press
7 Ellen Rd.
Middletown, RI 02842
stonetowerpress.com

Paperback ISBN: 978-1-7368651-7-0

Formatting and cover design by Amy Cole, JPL Design Solutions

Printed in the United States of America

DEDICATION

FROM WAYNE—

To Katya, thank you for all the help on this project.
You are my favorite daughter-in-law.

FROM JEREMY—

To Wayne, your partnership is a blessing.

To my 4, you make me a proud dad.

To Jenni, your enduring love while
I learn to write and teach is comforting.

CONTENTS

INTRODUCTION

In their covenant agreement beyond space-time and our knowledge, God the Father, Son, and Spirit deemed the Son would come to earth and rescue humans via His sacrificial death and resurrection. In that choice, it was determined that some man would serve as earthly father to the Son. Joseph was that choice. We know little about him, but everything we know points to a man of faith and obedience. These traits are precisely what every generation needs from those who go before them. As Scottish minister and theologian William Barclay summarized, "Jesus was growing up to boyhood, and then to manhood, in a good home; and there can be no greater start to life than that."[1]

St. Joseph and Jesus Child
by Vincenzo de Rossi

Matthew captures this faithfulness and obedience. Chapter 1 of his Gospel says of Joseph, "When Joseph woke up, he did as the Lord's angel had commanded him. He married her but did not have sexual relations with her until she gave birth to a son. And he named him Jesus." (vss 24–25) Chapter 2 verse 14 declares, "He [Joseph] got up, took the child and his mother during the night, and escaped to Egypt." Later, Matthew 2:21 relates how "He got up, took the child and his mother, and entered the land of Israel."[2]

Our goal in this brief study is to capture Joseph in words and principles half as well as Vincenzo de Rossi did in his magnificent 1547 marble sculpture that stands in the Roman Pantheon.[3] Strength, righteousness, and steadiness radiate from this man, whose massive hand is on the shoulder of young Jesus. Christians are called to sanctification, and the righteous earthly father of Jesus serves as an admirable guide as he builds his life around the Messiah, positively influences his family, and trusts God enough to obey fully. The story of Joseph also is a biblical reminder that in your family, or any family, you don't have to be a biological parent to be a parent who follows God's Word and biblical principles.

1
MARRY MARY

Having been honored to officiate over 150 weddings, we (Wayne and Jeremy) have collected some pretty unusual wedding stories—such as the time the pastor saw a bridesmaid about to pass out. She was swaying on the edge of a steep stage. He grabbed the groom, they ran down the steps, and arrived just in time to catch the girl as she fell back into their arms.

There also was the wedding of the very excited, perky bride whose ceremony was held in a small, historic venue. Candles were everywhere. It was beautiful. While Wayne was praying, the bride was bouncing, swinging her head back and forth. It was incredibly cute...until the back of her veil swung into the flame and caught on fire. Wayne reached over and grabbed the veil, wrapping the fabric in his hand until the little flare was extinguished. It only took a second or two and no one noticed as they were praying. Afterwards, he forgot all about it until one year later when the bride and groom were watching their wedding video for the first time. Wayne got a call during supper, and the bride shrieked as soon as he answered, "I was on fire! No one told me I was on fire!"

There are plenty of other hilarious moments, but as wild as our wonderful wedding stories are, we have never seen a wedding with as unexpected a twist as the one in Matthew 1!

A STAGE 1 PROBLEM

Matthew 1:18–19 informs us about Joseph and his betrothal to Mary:

> The birth of Jesus Christ came about this way: After his mother Mary had been engaged to Joseph, it was discovered before they came together that she was pregnant from the Holy Spirit. So her husband Joseph, being a righteous man, and not wanting to disgrace her publicly, decided to divorce her secretly. (CSB)

What Matthew describes is not like a modern engagement. Arnold Fruchtenbaum summarizes the situation nicely:

> This is a specified legal status...the Jewish marriage process involved two stages. The first stage is the engagement or betrothal, which, according to Bock, "involved a formal, witnessed agreement to marry and the giving of a bridal price. (Mal 2:14; *m. Ketubot* 4:4–5)." Legally, the woman...was then called the wife of [the husband-to-be], though the second stage of the marriage process, the ceremony itself, took place about a year later, when the groom took her home.[4]

The couple was formally "married" at this stage, though the ceremony and the consummation took place at some time later. Raymond Brown wrote a great book called *The Birth of the Messiah,* and he points out that because Mary and Joseph lived in Galilee, there is no way to get around the stigma of her pregnancy during stage 1 of marriage.[5] Thus, Matthew is detailing a "stage 1" problem.

Don't misunderstand. In the Roman Empire, an unexpected pregnancy was no big deal. A woman just got an abortion on her own, no permissions needed. As the famous Roman orator and statesman Cicero once lamented, "How multifaceted and aggressive are the abortioners' arts."[6]

But such wasn't the case in Jewish lands, and especially not in Galilee, where Joseph and Mary lived. Later Jewish commentary shows that in parts of Judea it was not unusual for the husband to be alone with his wife on at least one occasion in the interval between the two stages of marriage.[7] Yet in Galilee, no such leniency was tolerated. The wife had to be taken to her husband's home as a virgin. Therefore, Mary's pregnancy cannot be overlooked. Dr. Fruchtenbaum adds this:

> During this [stage 1 of marriage], only death or divorce could sever the contract, and a girl whose groom died during this period of waiting was referred to as a widow. The marriage ceremony lasted for seven days, and only *afterwards* was the marriage consummated.[8]

Mary and Joseph's whole world has been upended by her supernatural pregnancy. This is a stage 1 problem. And it's a topic that has received lots of study, usually from the perspective of Mary or her extended family. While that is useful, there is benefit as well in the far less-trammeled path of examining the Christmas story from the perspective of Joseph.

THE CHARACTER OF THE BRIDE

Before we learn more about Joseph and the couple's response to their stage 1 problem, let's get to know this bride whom Joseph has chosen. Much is known of Mary, but for our purposes today, there are two critical aspects we should note about the character of the bride.

First, Mary is a virgin. No author specifies for us the age of Mary at their betrothal. What they do say is that she is a virgin. Παρθένος, transliterated as *parthenos,* is the term used of her. It's a term never employed anywhere in Greek literature for a woman who has had sexual relations. *Parthenos* is used exclusively in reference to a virgin.

Jewish scholar Samuel Lachs points out that in John 8 the Pharisees unsuccessfully try to brand Jesus as a bastard. Lachs notes how Jesus laughs that off, using His virginal conception as proof of His deity. John records:

> [Jesus] "You're doing what your father does."
>
> [Pharisees] "We weren't born of sexual immorality," they said.
>
> "We have one Father—God."
>
> Jesus said to them, "If God were your Father, you would love me, because I came from God and I am here. For I didn't come on my own, but he sent me." (John 8:41–42)

Interestingly, the Pharisees abandon the bastard line of attack. Desperate, they shift to a different tack: "The Jews responded to him, 'Aren't we right in saying that you're a Samaritan and have a demon?'" (John 8:48) Intriguingly, they didn't go back to the illegitimate nonsense, because it was a dead end. *Everyone* knew better, just as everyone knew Jesus was neither demonized nor Samaritan. He was born of a virgin.[9]

Our culture laughs at virginity. It is a source of ridicule, in fact, much as it was in the Roman Empire of Joseph and Mary's day. Like the Jews in Galilee, Christians in America recognize the beauty and import of male and female virginity before marriage. But to the wider culture, virginity is absurd. And yet, it often seems that our culture, like the Roman one, laughs a bit too hard at biblical celibacy outside marriage. The jokes are so forced, the laughter so manic, that the mockery fails to hide their core cultural problem: objectification of humans. That is what lurks behind sexual promiscuity—selfishness that sees humans as merely material objects.

This promiscuity dynamic led the Roman Senator Cicero (106–43 BC) to give his fiery speech about the evils of abortion. He dared to say what no one wanted to admit—that widespread abortion in Rome went hand-in-glove with a false view of both humans and sexuality. Cicero was especially bothered by the way sexual promiscuity and abortion deeply wounded the economy. Mary is the opposite of what Cicero blasted. She is a virgin.

She is also a receiver of grace. That is the second aspect of Mary we must grasp; something Luke 1 reveals in verses 26–28:

> In the sixth month, the angel Gabriel was sent by God to a town in Galilee called Nazareth, to a virgin engaged to a man named Joseph, of the house of David. The virgin's name was Mary. And the angel came to her and said, "Greetings, favored woman! The Lord is with you."

Χαριτόω, *charitoo,* is the root word of what we render "favored woman." It signifies someone who has received the beneficent, undeserved favor of God. Interestingly, *charitoo* is only used at one other place in the Bible—Ephesians 1:6, where Paul writes, "to the praise of his glorious *grace,* with which he has blessed us in the Beloved."

This is very important. In each situation—with Mary in *Luke* and with all Christians in *Ephesians, charitoo* is the unmerited favor of God. Mary was favored by God, not inherently favoring herself. She needed to be blessed by God's grace just as we all do. Once again, Fruchtenbaum is spot on:

> She [Miriam, the Jewish rendering of her name] was being favored by God, she was receiving His grace; yet there is nothing in the text that even remotely implies that she herself was sinless...the Greek *kecharitomene* was translated into Latin as *gratia plena,* or "full of grace," as it is found in the Vulgate. Roman Catholicism developed from this the erroneous teaching that Miriam's fullness of grace allows her to bestow grace upon others. . . . this is not the biblical view. Miriam was a humble sinner, a truth she herself acknowledged when she said, *My spirit has rejoiced in God my Saviour* (Lk. 1:47). Only a sinful person needs a redeemer, so clearly, Miriam was not sinless.... God did not act because of her but on behalf of her.[10]

Though not a dispenser of grace, Mary teaches the most important thing one must grasp to prepare for eternity. Mary shows Joseph—and all of us—how to *receive* grace. Look at the passage referenced above—Luke 1:46–48:

> And Mary said:
> "My soul praises the greatness of the Lord,
> and my spirit rejoices in God my Savior,

because he has looked with favor
on the humble condition of his servant."

Her words are a brilliant primer on how to respond to God's grace. Mary's life pointed to the Messiah, not herself. Consider her declaration of "humble condition." That doesn't mean Mary thinks poorly of herself. It means she sees herself accurately. One cannot respond properly to God's grace without the bedrock comprehension that we are in need. No mere human is sinless. We are all separate from the Holy God.

Yet in that humility Mary teaches us to rejoice deep inside, in spirit, because the God who should only judge us has chosen to also rescue us! Messiah Jesus is God the Son, the Savior. That's why we can praise the greatness of the Lord. His advent on earth was a self-sacrificial rescue mission. Each human must respond to that truth.

THE CRISIS OF JOSEPH'S LIFE

Now, let's get back to the great crisis of Mary and Joseph's life together. "Secretly" is how the Christian Standard Bible describes Joseph's plan to divorce. Other translations render it "privately," but neither is exactly right. As a righteous man—meaning a Law-keeper—Joseph could not marry an unfaithful woman.

However, there was no legal way to keep such a thing *secret* or *private*. In Deuteronomy 24:1, Moses' law required a bill of divorce legally drawn up and accepted by the Elders of the village. There could be no secret divorce, especially as this law was clearly made to ensure that no woman could be abandoned or mistreated. To excuse any violation of Deuteronomy 24 sets an unacceptable precedent that removes one of God's protections for females in the covenant community.

What then does Matthew 1:19 mean? The biggest clue we have is the added clause, "not wanting to disgrace her publicly." The Jewish law contained provisions beyond mere divorce before Elders in the village gate. Numbers 5 declared adulterers could be publicly humiliated by an ordeal of a trial. If guilty, the person was stoned to death either by thrown rocks or being thrown off a cliff like the high one in Nazareth. (By the way, each method will figure later in Jesus' ministry.) It could be that Joseph was going to divorce Mary, but not disgrace her publicly by exposing her pregnancy and holding a public trial.

Thankfully, Joseph undergoes a reformation when God speaks directly to him through an angel, a vivid scene recorded in Matthew 1:20–25:

> But after he had considered these things, an angel of the Lord appeared to him in a dream, saying, "Joseph, son of David, don't be afraid to take Mary as your wife, because what has been conceived in her is from the Holy Spirit. She will give birth to a son, and you are to name him Jesus, because he will save his people from their sins."
>
> Now all this took place to fulfill what was spoken by the Lord through the prophet:
>
> *See, the virgin will become pregnant*
> *and give birth to a son,*
> *and they will name him Immanuel,*
> which is translated "God is with us."
>
> When Joseph woke up, he did as the Lord's angel had commanded him. He married her but did not have sexual relations with her until she gave birth to a son. And he named him Jesus.

This is obedience! The angel says to marry Mary and he does. He follows through with his marriage vow and brings on the stage 2 wedding ceremony.

Joseph's reaction is a complete shock. We expect to read Joseph saying, "This isn't fair! I have my own life to live." Or because he does trust YHWH, we anticipate a compromise statement from Joseph, "OK, I will do this. But only for a *while*. I am not going to have my whole life upended because God chose to bring a surprise child into the world." Such would be a normal response even from most God-followers. But Joseph is that rarest of souls—one who trusts God fully and obeys immediately.

God says the child is of the Holy Spirit, and not conceived immorally. Key in on that idea. The main issue in the text is God the Spirit. To feel the import of that pronouncement, we must perceive this revelation as Joseph would have understood Old Testament. For just a moment, set aside all you know of the Holy Spirit as revealed to and indwelling Christians. Think instead like a classical-era Jew. There are four things this revelation would have meant to Joseph:

- First, the Holy Spirit brought God's truth to humans. He inspired the prophets. He taught through Scripture. Therefore, this child Jesus will be the truth-bringer. Joseph would have understood what Dr. Barclay declared 1900 years later: "So then, Jesus is the one person who brings God's truth to men...Jesus is the one person who can tell us what God is like, and what God means us to be...Jesus came to tell us the truth about God and the truth about ourselves."[11] That's what "conceived of the Spirit" meant to Joseph.
- Second, the angel's speech indicated that at least some people would be enabled to recognize truth. Though

the doctrine of illumination is fully revealed in the New Testament, the idea begins in the Old Testament. People are blinded by sin and ignorance, and only the Holy Spirit working through God's Words can open those eyes. That means Jesus is the very Word of God. He is from the Spirit, which means He will enable people to see truth.

- Third, "of the Spirit" means that Jesus is Creator. The Hebrew Scriptures deeply connect the Spirit with the work of creation. (See texts such as Genesis 1, Job 33, Psalms 33 and 104.) The New Testament will pick up on this. In fact, Colossians reveals how Jesus is fully Creator of the Universe.
- Fourth, the Holy Spirit is the agent of re-creation. Ezekiel shows that God the Spirit will bring the dead back to life and restore all creation. That explains a popular rabbinic saying of the 1st century: "God says to Israel: In this world my Spirit has put wisdom in you, but in the future my Spirit will make you live again."[12]

Those four points are present in the message from God's angel, and all that is at least partly grasped by Joseph, who must have been astounded at this verbiage. Two other linguistic bombs are dropped in this text: the angel declares this is all fulfillment of Isaiah 7 and God says to name the baby Jesus. We'll shelve those for now, examining each in depth in later chapters. Just keep those two bombshells on the back burner. For now, note that Joseph does *exactly* what God commands.

Amazing! In Joseph, we meet someone who truly trusts God's words and follows them in practical obedience. We pray the same can be said of us. We pray that by God's grace, change will be accomplished in our lives such that we are obedient and faithful like Joseph.

In 1886, D. L. Moody was leading a series of evangelistic meetings in Massachusetts. The music director, Ira Sankey, was impressed with one young man who stood up and testified, saying, "I don't understand everything. But I am going to trust. And I am going to obey." Sankey shared that testimony with a friend of his named John Sammis. Rev. Sammis was a Presbyterian pastor who had just joined the faculty of the school now known as Biola University. Sammis wrote a poem around the testimony, which begins this way:

> When we walk with the Lord
> in the light of his word,
> what a glory he sheds on our way!
> what he says we will do,
> where he sends we will go;
> never fear, only trust and obey.[13]

When John Sammis sent the poem back to his pal in Boston, Sankey soon added music to the lyrics. Some of you grew up singing the hymn. There are few humans that "Trust and Obey" describes better than Joseph.

Wayne vividly remembers a time when his divergence from Joseph was laid bare. Church had just concluded with "Trust and Obey" serving as the closing hymn. As usual, a gaggle of high school guys gathered in the section of foyer they claimed as private territory. From this lyceum, teenage Wayne and his friends pontificated about theology, music, and sports, confident no group had ever possessed the philosophical and practical wisdom they embodied. The conversations were often delightful despite generational hubris, and this particular Sunday they discussed that campy old song which had ended church. Their conclusion was that "Trust and Obey" possesses great meaning; that even though it was old and old people sang it too often, the lyrics were solid.

The guys dispersed, drawn away by the insatiable youthful desire for food. A few minutes later, Wayne was in the passenger seat as his best buddy ran a stop sign. He broke the law without a thought, compelled to arrive at the restaurant in time for his parents to pay for lunch. As they sped down the little street in Bethany, Oklahoma, Wayne would likely have thought nothing of their disobedient violation of Romans 13; however, he was still humming "Trust and Obey." Suddenly, conviction descended, deeply. Wayne shared with his buddy, who frowned and slowed down. They rode in silence to the restaurant.

THE NORMAL COURSE OF GALILEAN FAMILY LIFE

Our other lessons in this study will expand on Joseph's beautiful, powerful trust and obedience. To make certain we get full benefit from those lessons, let's spend a moment on the normal course of Galilean family life.

A child's weaning normally occurred before 2 years of age. Like every part of Jewish life, the rabbis had rules for this, and 2 years was the absolute latest for weaning. Later, years after the life and death and resurrection of Jesus, another set of rabbinic rules allowed up to 5 years of milk feeding, but only if the child had been continuously fed exclusively on milk. (Wayne has read the treatises and cannot figure out what was behind the new allowance. We guess the earliest La Leche League had a strong rabbinic lobby!)

After weaning and a few years at home, every child entered school, which was held in the synagogue. The Hebrews were the first people to ever practice compulsory public education. Like all great education, it began at home. Devotional Scriptures were discussed at home with every child during his or her first 5 years. At 5, strong students began *bet safer*—what we would call elementary school. All others started by 7 years old. Instruction began in Leviticus, as it dealt with ritual purity and maintaining healthy community.

Did you attend a religious, parochial, Christian, or madras school? If so, you may have memories of harsh teachers with punishing rules. Fascinatingly, that was not anything like the Jewish synagogue school. Rabbis were carefully chosen, and only the most patient and talented teachers were given school posts.

Extant letters from the time show that students loved their teaching rabbis. They taught the students through outdoor activities, Scripture memorization, wider reading, writing, and apparently some arithmetic. As far as we can tell, most children enjoyed school, even the ones who weren't good at it. But that doesn't mean there weren't rules! Here were the main policies:

- The rabbi holds "kingship" over the school.
- Students stand until invited to sit.
- A student cannot leave without permission.
- All stand when the teacher enters or leaves.
- The teacher is only called "Rabbi."
- School meets seven days a week, except for harvest. On Shabbat, students review all learned during the week.[14]

Speaking of Sabbath, Alfred Edersheim pointed out something moving:

> One might assume that synagogue, as the place of worship, would be considered more important or more sacred than the schools, but this was not the case. To this day, the bet midrash is given more prominence than the synagogue—not because education is valued more highly than worship, but because Judaism does not make a distinction between the two. Indeed, Judaism has always held that study of Torah is one of the highest forms of worship.[15]

When a student turned 10, he or she could enter the *bet midrash*—secondary school—where older students and some adults studied Torah and rabbinic traditions. At 12 or13, a student was considered subject to the commandments—the age of accountability for what they had been learning.

At that point, most went to work and only attended school on occasion. Their work was usually an apprenticeship. If apprenticed to the father's profession, they stayed at home until at least 18. Sometimes, a youth would be apprenticed to someone else, who then had responsibility for their care until 18. At that age, the apprenticeship was usually considered complete, and the young man could become a part-owner in a business. At 30, they were considered a person of full strength. Priests, for example, could not serve until age 30.

However, there was an alternate path that branched at the age of accountability. At 13, a few truly outstanding students left home and studied with a famous rabbi. This peripatetic study was somewhat similar to the Greek style of following a philosopher around; however, the Hebrew method focused on application of Scripture and not merely on logic. Male students could apply for this position. If accepted, they left home to travel with and learn from the rabbi. Many families would support their youth on this adventure. Sometimes, men older than 18 would choose to follow and study with a rabbi. They usually sold their business or left it with family.

THE SPECIAL CIRCUMSTANCES OF JOSEPH AND MARY'S FAMILY LIFE

Speaking of family and adventure, let's look briefly at the special circumstances of Joseph and Mary's family life. They were in a singular situation. However bright and delightful our offspring, most of us don't have to raise truly different children. Of course, some do. Some get to rear children with what the world calls severe disabilities. Others get to shepherd almost supernaturally gifted athletes and artists. Still others are cursed—that is, blessed—with guiding children that are unbelievably intelligent.

Yet no one has ever had to face what Joseph and Mary experienced. They had to rear God the Son! Joseph had to be earthly father/stepfather to a boy conceived of the Holy Spirit! In a meager attempt to understand, we conducted an informal survey with a few great parents who have the burden and blessing of parenting a very gifted child. We asked, "On what do you rely in order to successfully rear your precocious child?" These were the responses:

- Other parents
- Youth leaders
- Antacids
- Grandparents
- Schools
- God

That last one is where we can learn much from Jesus' family. You see, Jesus—fully human—was blessed to learn directly from God the Father. Five hundred years before the birth of Jesus, Isaiah prophesied how this would occur:

> The Lord God has given me
> the tongue of those who are instructed
> to know how to sustain the weary with a word.
> He awakens me each morning;
> he awakens my ear to listen like those being instructed.
> The Lord God has opened my ear,
> and I was not rebellious;
> I did not turn back.
> I gave my back to those who beat me,
> and my cheeks to those who tore out my beard.
> I did not hide my face from scorn and spitting.
> The Lord God will help me;
> therefore I have not been humiliated;
> therefore I have set my face like flint,
> and I know I will not be put to shame. (Isaiah 50:4–7)

This describes special training that came directly from God. Jesus, the human boy, had direct instruction from the words of God the Father.

Before we delve into that, let's take a moment and apply this to all our children and grandchildren, nieces and nephews. The most important thing one can do is teach that child how to engage directly with God's Word. Your input is significant, but it isn't most important. Neither is that expensive coach or special experience critical for the child's development. Those things are all fine, but the #1 factor for grit and success is to train a child to follow God's words.

Regarding the special child-rearing issues here from Joseph's perspective, let's listen to Dr. Fruchtenbaum again. This is brilliant:

> Morning by morning, God the Father awakened His Son and took Him aside to disciple Him, to train Him, to teach Him who He is and what His mission was to be (Isa. 50:4). Yeshua is a unique individual; He is the God-Man....He is only one person, but He has two distinct natures: a divine nature and a human nature. These two natures exist side by side; they never mixed. While in His deity, He is omniscient; in His humanity, He had to undergo the same type of learning experience that all humans have to undergo....God the Father did that by waking Him up morning by morning to train Him in matters concerning His person, His message, and His work. Even when He realized that His mission included suffering and death, He was not rebellious (Isa. 50:5)....When the time came for Him to fulfill His mission, He gave His *back to the smiters*...(Isa 50:6). Furthermore, He gave His *cheeks to them that plucked off the hair* [*of His beard* and] did not cover His face from the spittle being spat upon Him. He *set His face like a flint* to fulfill His mission (Isa. 50:7)....as a result of this training by God the Father, at the age of 12 Yeshua knew exactly who He was: the Son of God. He also knew the Scriptures so well that He was able to debate them with the scholars in the Temple compound.[16]

That journey to Jerusalem and the Temple contains another scene we'll mine in depth later. For now, just catch this: Joseph and Mary took Jesus to the Temple as the Law instructed. Even though God the Father trained Jesus the Son, His human parents took him on many journeys designed to protect Him and instruct Him.

Without a doubt they *sacrificed* to do this! Joseph surrendered steady work and career advancement. Each parent surrendered family relationships and reputations. It's evident that their whole lives were built around being great parents to the God-Man King; which takes us to two huge application questions:

- Will I submit to the Triune God; i.e., trust and obey?
- Will I accept the calling of living with my everything pointing to Messiah?

That's what Joseph did when he married Mary. It's what Mary did in response to the angel Gabriel. It's what they both achieved in the normal and extraordinary aspects of raising their son. They obeyed, submitting to God. They accepted the incredible, counter-intuitive fullness of a life where everything was about Jesus. Every part of life was changed to point to Messiah.

The same challenge is placed before every one of us.

2

GET UP!

STRESS AND OBEDIENCE

How did Joseph respond to stress and what does it mean for us?

The first definition of *stress* in *The Merriam-Webster Dictionary* reads:

> stress noun\'stres
>
> constraining force or influence such as
>
> a: a force exerted when one body or body part presses on, pulls on, pushes against, or tends to compress or twist another body or body part; *especially* the intensity of this mutual force commonly expressed in pounds per square inch
>
> b: the deformation caused in a body by such a force
>
> c: a physical, chemical, or emotional factor that causes bodily or mental tension and may be a factor in disease causation

> d: a state resulting from a stress; *especially*: one of bodily or mental tension resulting from factors that tend to alter an existent equilibrium; job-related *stress*

Jeremy illustrated this definition rather dramatically. Here's how he summarized the experience in a recent presentation:

> It was a dark and stormy night. Seriously! I was driving the family to a school concert for one of the kids and dropped everyone off as close to the door as possible to make their trek through the rain a little shorter. I parked the car and decided to jog toward the auditorium in order to get out of the rain faster. Never mind the fact that there is this cool new invention called an umbrella that is designed to help keep rain off of you. I didn't need that kind of help and left our umbrella in the car.
>
> The rain was actually letting up as I jogged into the building. Suddenly, I began to slip on the wet pavement and as I slid, my foot came in contact with something that immediately stopped all forward inertia of said foot. The rest of the body continued in motion. This lasted only a second, until my body experienced a sharp jolt and an audible snap.
>
> In that split-second, my mind recognized that said foot was now facing the wrong direction! So, I collapsed to the ground in an effort to avoid more damage. As I lay there in the light sprinkle, I wondered, "What just happened?"

In the words from the spiritual "Dem Bones" (inspired by Ezekiel 37:1–4) written by the brilliant writer, lyricist, and civil rights activist James Weldon Johnson, "your ankle bone" is no longer "connected to your shin bone."[17] For more anatomically-minded people, the tibia and fibula extend downward connecting to the bones that comprise the foot. The stress placed on Jeremy's ankle connections snapped both those bones. The tibia and fibula broke, dislocated forward, and crushed part of the talus bone. With his foot stopped in its place, the pressure being applied by the rest of the body in motion overcame whatever strength was present in the bones and snapped them apart. The lack of alignment bowed to stress and broke Jeremy's lower leg and ankle bones.

After surgical repair, we were looking in awe at Jeremy's Emergency Room x-ray. Jeremy commented, "This serves as a picture of our spiritual condition at times." When questioned about stressful things in our lives, most of us respond with answers like:

- relationship pains
- a bad boss who makes unreasonable demands
- difficult financial realities
- injury or sickness
- loving difficult family members (especially at holiday gatherings)
- unreliable employees
- taxes and regulations
- concern you are underachieving

This list is not exhaustive, of course. Here between Garden and Heaven, there are manifold ways that humans are pressed and pulled and pushed. Sometimes the stressors are freakish—like the seemingly impossible twist when Jeremy's foot somehow fixated on wet pavement. Often the stresses of life are more mundane. Yet in every situation, the important question isn't, "What just happened?" The most significant question is, "What should I do now?"

In Jeremy's case, immediately after he wondered "What just happened?" he prayed. Calmed, he answered, "Yes!" to the lady asking if she needed to call 911. When the kind man kneeling next to him offered to call his wife, Jeremy realized Jenni wasn't going to answer the unknown number. So, he wiggled around to retrieve his phone from his soaking pocket, dialed the number, and handed it to the man to tell her she needed to come outside. The paramedics arrived rapidly, horrified to find the man they respect as their Fire Department Chaplain lying in the rain with "his leg on backwards." They rapidly and professionally stabilized their chaplain and rushed him to surgery.

Whether physical or non-material, every life crisis demands that kind of response. In the moment of stress and danger, one must focus and act on what should be done now to realign. Even when the situation isn't life-threatening, mishandled pressure becomes a thief of joy. Trying to avoid the inherent pain leads people to do things that are harmful to self and others. Pouting over misfortune makes for bitterness and blame. In summary, if we don't learn to handle stress wisely, we will prove ineffective and possibly dangerous—to ourselves, our communities, and the work of God.

Studying Joseph, the man God chose to be the earthly father of the Messiah while he grew up on earth, our minds almost inevitably turn to Christmas. It is the only season when most people give Joseph even a passing thought. Many people in western cultures find the Christmas season extremely stressful. We certainly don't want to make light of any struggles, but the stress Joseph experienced might help put things in perspective for us. Leading up to the first Christmas and during the period following Jesus' birth, Jesus' earthly father dealt with pressures that make a compound fracture seem routine. Joseph decided to handle the stress by trusting and obeying God, aligning with God's decrees, covenants, and commands.

Joseph proves to be one of the most obedient people in recorded history. Faced with a significant succession of stressful situations, Jesus' foster father trusts God's word and obeys fully each and every time.

JOSEPH OBEYED GOD'S NAME DECREE.

Let's again read Matthew 1:20–25

> But after he had considered these things, an angel of the Lord appeared to him in a dream, saying, "Joseph, son of David, don't be afraid to take Mary as your wife, because what has been conceived in her is from the Holy Spirit. She will give birth to a son, and you are to name him Jesus, because he will save his people from their sins."
>
> Now all this took place to fulfill what was spoken by the Lord through the prophet:
>
> *See, the virgin will become pregnant*
> *and give birth to a son,*
> *and they will name him Immanuel,*
> which is translated "God is with us."
>
> When Joseph woke up, he did as the Lord's angel had commanded him. He married her but did not have sexual relations with her until she gave birth to a son. And he named him Jesus.

We saw before that Joseph trusted and obeyed when he followed the Lord's command to marry Mary. Now he once again works through the stressful situation by submitting to the Lord's decree and naming the baby Jesus, a name also rendered Yeshua and Joshua. To name the baby this represents a fun wordplay in Hebrew: *You shall call his name Yeshua for it is he that shall yoshia (save) his people from their sins.*

Names in Scripture are designed to capture the person's essential self—their life, purpose, and ethic. To name a baby Yeshua/Joshua/Jesus is a massive statement. It is to say that this is the Messiah. This is the one who will save those who trust YHWH. Joseph could have been ashamed of this child, given all the fuss and stress. Instead, he proudly proclaimed salvation in His name.

Joseph followed the word of the Lord and named the baby Jesus. Amid an incredibly stressful situation, his trust and obedience exemplify what it means to not be ashamed of the good news. Romans 1:16 expands and applies this concept, declaring, "For I am not ashamed of the gospel, because it is the power of God for salvation to everyone who believes, first to the Jew, and also to the Greek."

Is that true of each of us? One way to assess is to ask yourself, "How faithfully am I proclaiming the good news of Jesus when things are not going my way?" When the pressures of life are bearing down from all sides; when I am physically, emotionally, or spiritually broken down, is the first thought in my mind and heart to proclaim the truth of His name—that He, Jesus, is the way, the truth, and the life?

Joseph named the baby *Jesus* just as God decreed, proclaiming the arrival of the Messiah. Even in a painful, confusing, embarrassing situation, Joseph remained steadfast in his faith and declared salvation in the name of Jesus.

JOSEPH OBEYED GOD'S COVENANTS.

Luke 2 shows how Joseph's respect for God's word extended to the covenantal decrees. Verse 21 tells us that "When the eight days were completed for his circumcision, he was named Jesus—the name given by the angel before he was conceived."

Again, no one explains the details from a Hebrew perspective as well as Arnold Fruchtenbaum:

> Circumcision was commanded under two of the five Jewish covenants: the Abrahamic covenant and the Mosaic Covenant. However, in each case, the meaning was a bit different. Under the Abrahamic Covenant, circumcision was a sign of the covenant and a sign of Jewishness. Under the Mosaic Covenant, circumcision was the means of submitting to the law. Under the Abrahamic Covenant, it was mandatory for Jews only, and those who were permanent residents within a Jewish household. Under the Mosaic Covenant, it was mandatory for both Jews and those Gentiles who wished to become part of the commonwealth of Israel. Because it was the means of submitting to the laws, Paul warned the Gentile Galatians that if they submitted to circumcision, it would obligate them to keep the whole law, not just that one commandment of the law.[18]

It's important to remember that circumcision wasn't merely part of the Mosaic Covenant. It is older, a part of the eternal, unconditional Abrahamic Covenant. Moses' Law covenant was temporary and conditional. By contrast, the Abrahamic Covenant is ongoing, and Joseph's engagement with that covenant is exposed through a surprising twist. Joseph and Mary followed the Mosaic Law requirement to bring their firstborn to the Temple for dedication to the Lord. While they were at the Temple in obedience, they witnessed an amazing scene and received an unexpected blessing.

> And when the days of their purification according to the law of Moses were finished, they brought him up to Jerusalem to present him to the Lord (just as it is written in the law of the Lord, *Every firstborn male will be dedicated to the Lord*) and to offer a sacrifice (according to what is stated in the law of the Lord, *a pair of turtledoves or two young pigeons.*)
>
> There was a man in Jerusalem whose name was Simeon. This man was righteous and devout, looking forward to Israel's consolation, and the Holy Spirit was on him.
>
> It had been revealed to him by the Holy Spirit that he would not see death before he saw the Lord's Messiah.
>
> Guided by the Spirit, he entered the temple. When the parents brought in the child Jesus to perform for him what was customary under the law, Simeon took him up in his arms, praised God, and said,
>
> Now, Master,
> you can dismiss your servant in peace,
> as you promised.
> For my eyes have seen your salvation.
> You have prepared it
> in the presence of all peoples—
> a light for revelation to the Gentiles and glory to your people Israel.
>
> His father and mother were amazed at what was being said about him.
>
> Then Simeon blessed them and told his mother Mary: "Indeed, this child is destined to cause the fall and rise of many

> in Israel and to be a sign that will be opposed—and a sword will pierce your own soul—that the thoughts of many hearts may be revealed." (Luke 2:22–35)

When Joseph and Mary dutifully take Jesus to the Temple, Simeon, who isn't mentioned anywhere else in Scripture, also enters the Temple. He isn't there by accident. Rather, he is a man who himself trusts and obeys the Lord. As Joseph and Mary enter the Temple, the focus is on the Mosaic Law covenant—thus the quotes from Moses. But Simeon turns the whole scene into an affirmation of Abraham's covenant with God. Seeing Jesus, Simeon scooped up the child, looked salvation in the eyes, and made his remarkable claim that this child would be "a light for revelation to the Gentiles and glory to your people Israel." His declaration about Jesus is Abrahamic, as that covenant promises that all the world—including Gentiles—will be blessed through Abraham's offspring.

Isn't that beautiful? Joseph and Mary thought so. Look again at verse following Simeon's proclamation: "His father and mother were amazed at what was being said about him."

Have you ever been amazed by someone praising your children or praying profound truth over them? Parents, grandparents, and extended family treasure such experiences. It brings joy when someone else proclaims the greatness of your family, and it's even more encouraging when that praise is unexpected. Joseph and Mary knew who Jesus was. They knew He was to be great, but nowhere does Scripture say that they knew every detail of what was supposed to happen. Nor does the text even imply they knew exactly how to raise the Messiah. Yet because they simply trusted and obeyed in God's covenants, they were encouraged and blessed while attending to their parental duty in the Temple.

There is always blessing in obedience, and Jesus' faithful earthly father was blessed in circumcising the child and holding fast to the Abrahamic Covenant of living righteously by faith. Those who believe in Jesus are made righteous by faith as part of the continuing Abrahamic Covenant now revealed in the work of Jesus the resurrected Messiah. How about us? Are we each walking by faith and doing what is right before the Lord as Joseph did?

JOSEPH OBEYED GOD'S CALLS TO MOVE.

The faithful stepfather of Jesus obeyed in naming the Messiah as God decreed, he obeyed God's covenants, and he obeyed God's calls to move his family. In Matthew 2, an angel tells Joseph to flee with his family to Egypt, and he does so.

> After they [the magi] were gone, an angel of the Lord appeared to Joseph in a dream, saying, "Get up! Take the child and his mother, flee to Egypt, and stay there until I tell you. For Herod is about to search for the child to kill him."
>
> So he got up, took the child and his mother during the night, and escaped to Egypt.
>
> He stayed there until Herod's death, so that what was spoken by the Lord through the prophet might be fulfilled: *Out of Egypt I called my Son.*
>
> Then Herod, when he realized that he had been outwitted by the wise men, flew into a rage. He gave orders to massacre all the boys in and around Bethlehem who were two years old and under, in keeping with the time he had learned from the wise men.
>
> Then what was spoken through Jeremiah the prophet was fulfilled:

> *A voice was heard in Ramah,*
> *weeping, and great mourning,*
> *Rachel weeping for her children;*
> *and she refused to be consoled,*
> *because they are no more.* (Matthew 2:13–18)

The newborn king's life was in danger and Joseph, by an angel, was told what to do to care for him: "Get up and go." Beyond the life-threatening danger from Herod, there are at least of couple of other pressing realities that almost surely plagued the young family. They were poor. Otherwise, Luke would have stated that they offered a lamb, not the poverty-level sacrifice of two birds. Though the magi gave lovely gifts, we have no idea of the quantities. These may have been only token amounts. Thankfully, those gifts could be sold for cash, as Joseph would have been unable to work at his trade for a good part of the journeys. Further, every young family in any age can testify to the labor involved in travelling a good distance with a child, especially on short notice. We sometimes find hardship in a road trip with a child in an air-conditioned car going 60 miles per hour. One can only imagine what a foot journey to the Roman province of Egypt entailed.

It's significant that Egypt was fully a province of the Republic [Note: it would be a few more years before the Romans began to think of their world as an "empire," and more still before they would readily refer to it as such.] As an official province, Egypt was beyond Herod's reach. Once Herod was gone, the family was called to move again. Matthew continues:

> After Herod died, an angel of the Lord appeared in a dream to Joseph in Egypt, saying, "Get up, take the child and his mother, and go to the land of Israel, because those who intended to kill

> the child are dead." So he got up, took the child and his mother, and entered the land of Israel. (Matthew 2:19–21)

Thomas Constable shares this great insight:

> God's sovereign initiative is again the subject of Matthew's record. This is the fourth dream and the third mention of the angel of the Lord appearing to Joseph in the prologue. The phrase *the land of Israel* occurs only here in the New Testament. Evidently Matthew used it since it recalls the promises and blessings God gave Jacob and his descendants.[19]

Every time, Joseph gets up and goes. Ever the faithful father, Joseph hears the Word from the Lord, trusts His promises and blessings, and obeys His directives. In fact, Matthew recounts that God has one more opportunity for Joseph to live by faith"

> But when he [Joseph] heard that Archelaus was ruling over Judea in place of his father Herod, he was afraid to go there. And being warned in a dream, he withdrew to the region of Galilee. Then he went and settled in a town called Nazareth to fulfill what was spoken through the prophets, that he [Messiah] would be called a Nazarene. (Matthew 2:22–23)

William Barclay relates this important background about the situation after Herod's death, and why Joseph was right to be afraid:

> When Herod died the whole kingdom over which he had ruled was split up. The Romans had trusted Herod, and they had allowed him to reign over a very considerable territory, but

> Herod well knew that none of his sons would be allowed a like power. So he had divided his kingdom into three, and in his will he had left a part to each of his three sons, He had left Judaea to Archelaus; he had left Galilee to Herod Antipas; and he had left the region away to the north-east and beyond Jordan to Philip. But the death of Herod did not solve the problem. Archelaus was a bad king and he was not to last long on the throne. In point of fact he had begun his reign with an attempt to out-Herod Herod, for he had opened his rule with the deliberate slaughter of three thousand of the most influential people in the country. Clearly, even now that Herod was dead, it was still unsafe to return to Judaea with the savage and reckless Archelaus on the throne.[20]

Once again, Joseph simply trusted and obeyed what the Lord told him to do and went to Nazareth. Regardless of the pressure surrounding him, Joseph got up and went where he was supposed to go. Regardless of the stress that he could have used as an excuse to numb himself, lash out, or collapse in understandable self-pity, he got up.

STRESS AND REALIGNMENT

When we met to work on this chapter, Jeremy was recovering from surgery on his leg and ankle. Sitting in a wheelchair, he began to laugh. It had been some time since we had worked on this book, and each of us had forgotten the next chapter before us already had been given the working title "Get Up!" When he reminded Wayne, we shared a good laugh at the irony and decided that title was perfect. Getting up isn't always physical, but it is always important. (Note for any concerned: as of printing time,

Jeremy has completed physical therapy and is walking, leaping, and praising God.)

Stress is a normal part of life. There are pressures that push, pull, and twist us. There are demands which, if not relieved, can render us ineffective in life. We must get realigned. Humans are always searching for ways to relieve the stress. From religious systems to healthcare and beauty products, people will seemingly buy into anything that promises to make the pain go away. (Seriously. Jeremy's daughters have shampoo and lotion that claims to offer "Stress Relief.")

Can a lotion take the pains of life away? Perhaps it can help a bit temporarily at moments, but no stress-relieving lotion would have stopped Jeremy's ankle from breaking. Nor will a nice smelling shampoo remove the hurt springing from the loss of a loved one. No Eastern meditation or yoga eliminates the difficulty of working for a mean-spirited boss. No matter how sweetly scented, a soap won't clean nor change our sinful hearts.

So how does one find relief from the stress? How can we thrive when the pressures surround us? It's actually very simple, and the faithful stepfather of Jesus is a great example to us. The ultimate stress reliever is to trust and obey. What must give is our attempts of controlling the situations in our lives based on our own power.

Think of your life like Jeremy's foot. When it lodged unmoving on the concrete, it became out of alignment with the body. It had to quickly realign or face a painful break. Had it come unstuck, Jeremy would have merely rolled in the puddles and moved on, wet, but none the worse for wear. Because the foot didn't budge, the bones had to be realigned via surgery. It was a much more difficult path, but effective. True, a great deal of agony could have been avoided by immediate obedience, but alignment was achieved in the end.

In a similar way, each Christian is part of the body over which God reigns as head. When we are feeling stress, it grants a perfect opportunity to check whether we are aligned with His instructions. Often, we are not. Sometimes, we respond too late to avoid a fracture. Other times, the break is—like Jeremy's jog—beyond our responsibility. Yet in each case God wonderfully serves as the Great Physician. He repairs us, bringing us into line with His decrees, covenant, and callings.

Our prayer is that each of us will respond immediately, as did Joseph, thus enjoying unbroken fellowship with God. If your fellowship with the Lord seems to be breaking, submit to His word immediately! Roll with the stress and get up. If you are emerging from a season of realignment and repair, spend less thought on "What just happened?" and more on "What do I do now?" Get up and do the spiritual therapy necessary to strengthen your soul.

3

GUIDE THE GOD-MAN KING

COLD CLAY

Since he first viewed it years ago, Wayne has been smitten with Vincenzo de Rossi's statue of Joseph that stands guard in the Roman Pantheon. Through the centuries, there have been other Joseph-themed works of art, some of them excellent. A recent favorite is Mary-Patrice Woehling's poem:

> He scrubbed the trough and filled it with fresh hay.
> The midnight sky was bright and hard and raw;
> The constellations danced above cold clay.
>
> That night the heavens put on a display
> That froze wise man and shepherd mute with awe.
> He scrubbed the trough and filled it with fresh hay

And wondered how long they would have to stay
In Bethlehem fulfilling Caesar's law.
That night the heavens put on a display

While Herod hoped the Magi would betray
The child sleeping snugly in the straw.
He scrubbed the trough and filled it with fresh hay,

Too cold and busy to kneel down to pray;
His fingers, stiff and wet, would need to thaw.
That night the heavens put on a display

While Joseph worked and watched as Mary lay
And nursed the baby. Sheep and oxen saw
He scrubbed the trough and filled it with fresh hay;
The constellations danced above cold clay.[21]

We were especially taken with the cadence that builds power in the tempo. Joseph's strong hands are preparing for Messiah. His focus is not on self, but exclusively on Jesus. Notice also the context to Joseph's focus: "the heavens put on a display" and "constellations danced" but on earth is "cold clay." What a brilliant image! Cold clay and dancing heaven are particularly significant for understanding Joseph in context.

BACKGROUND ON MESSIAH'S PROMISE

To understand the context more fully, we need to start further back in biblical history with the Davidic line and prophecies. The prince of the prophets, Isaiah, provides an excellent summary in Isaiah 7:

This took place during the reign of Ahaz, son of Jotham, son of Uzziah king of Judah: Aram's King Rezin and Israel's King Pekah son of Remaliah went to fight against Jerusalem, but they were not able to conquer it.

When it became known to the house of David that Aram had occupied Ephraim, the heart of Ahaz and the hearts of his people trembled like trees of a forest shaking in the wind.

The LORD said to Isaiah, "Go out with your son Shear-jashub to meet Ahaz at the end of the conduit of the upper pool, by the road to the Launderer's Field.

Say to him: Calm down and be quiet. Don't be afraid or cowardly because of these two smoldering sticks, the fierce anger of Rezin and Aram, and the son of Remaliah. For Aram, along with Ephraim and the son of Remaliah, has plotted harm against you. They say, 'Let us go up against Judah, terrorize it, and conquer it for ourselves. Then we can install Tabeel's son as king in it.'"

This is what the Lord GOD says:

It will not happen; it will not occur.
The chief city of Aram is Damascus,
the chief of Damascus is Rezin
(within sixty-five years
Ephraim will be too shattered to be a people),
the chief city of Ephraim is Samaria,
and the chief of Samaria is the son of Remaliah.
If you do not stand firm in your faith,
then you will not stand at all.

Then the LORD spoke again to Ahaz: "Ask for a sign from the LORD your God—it can be as deep as Sheol or as high as heaven."

But Ahaz replied, "I will not ask. I will not test the LORD."
Isaiah said,

> "Listen, house of David! Is it not enough for you to try the patience of men? Will you also try the patience of my God? Therefore, the Lord himself will give you a sign: See, the virgin will conceive, have a son, and name him Immanuel. By the time he learns to reject what is bad and choose what is good, he will be eating curds and honey. For before the boy knows to reject what is bad and choose what is good, the land of the two kings you dread will be abandoned. The LORD will bring on you, your people, and your father's house such a time as has never been since Ephraim separated from Judah: He will bring the king of Assyria."

This passage contains a fascinating double reference, meaning two prophesies are being revealed. Isaiah 7:2 describes Israel (the northern part of the divided Israeli kingdoms) and Syria (often called Aram) combining to destroy not only King Ahaz of Judah, but all the house of David. They were trying to eliminate all the line of David that has the right to reign from Jerusalem.

In verse 3, Isaiah is sent by God to meet Ahaz. In verses 4–6, he describes the plot and tells Ahaz to not fear. As encouragement, Isaiah takes along his son, whose name means "A remnant will return." In verse 6, Isaiah—a Hebrew genius—plays on the name of the usurper planned for the Davidic throne. Tabeel means "God is good." Isaiah altered the vowels to describe Tabeel's son as "good for nothing." Any conspiracy to topple the Davidic Covenant is good for nothing.

In summary, Syria and the northern Jewish kingdom of Israel are conspiring to destroy the southern kingdom of Judah and the entire line of David. It won't work, because they are good for nothing and a remnant will always return.

With that in mind, let's consider the signs. God pushes Ahaz to ask for a sign. This is not the biblical norm, and it seems really odd until you consider the character and actions of Ahaz. King Ahaz is a liar who thinks he can fool God. Prior to this encounter, Ahaz had been sending letters and gifts to Assyria, begging the Assyrian emperor for help against the conspiracy of kings. God thus offers a miracle to convince Ahaz to trust YHWH instead of Assyria.

The best moment is when Ahaz, a serial idolater, suddenly remembers Deuteronomy 6:16 and rejects the offer of a sign. The tone carries the smugness of a person committed to wrong who is for once doing something right. But Ahaz's attempt at nobility is misguided. Deuteronomy commands people not to *ask* for a sign. *Receiving* an offered one is different. So, God gives signs, despite Ahaz' fake protest.

For the first sign, in verses 13–14, God shifts to a plural "you," signifying all Israel. Everything up to that had been a singular "you," referencing Ahaz or Isaiah. This shift is not visible in English, but it makes a huge difference. "See" or "Behold" in verse 14 is a term that can call attention to an event past, present, or future. When used with a present participle, as here, it always indicates a future event. Thus, Immanuel's conception and birth described in verse 14 are future from Ahaz's perspective. All Judah would have understood this as prophecy intended for all.

Further, verse 14 uses the definite article "the" virgin. Because no immediate virgin is mentioned, the "principle of previous/common reference" must be employed. The only virginal birth reference known by all Jews was Genesis 3:15, where all humanity is promised that the woman's seed would bring salvation. The fact that *man's* seed is notably left out was very important. Many rabbis declared that Genesis 3 indicated a future miraculous virginal conception and birth.

Arnold Fruchtenbaum aptly notes:

> The key point of this should not be missed. God was promising that the House of David could not be deposed or lose its identity until the birth of a virgin-born son. This was clearly future [from Ahaz's day] and would require that the Messiah be born prior to the destruction of the Temple and its genealogical records in A.D. 70.[22]

Dancing heaven will interact with cold clay with the arrival of Immanuel, God with us. That is one of the two prophecies spoken to Ahaz. The second promise starts at verse 15, where the text switches back to a singular "you."

The first promise, that the line of David would be fulfilled in a virgin-born son, used the plural "you." It was a statement for all of Judah forever. This second promise comes with a textual shift. The "you" becomes singular again. It is directed only to King Ahaz.

Also, there is a definite article "the" before "he." That can only mean Isaiah's son, as he is the only *boy* mentioned in the context. This is not a *baby* as in the first prophecy. God is declaring that Israel and Syria will have their kings deposed before Shear-jashub reaches the age of accountability, which in that era was about the age of 12 years old.

In summary, there are two prophetic promises in Isaiah 7:

- All Judah is prophesied a deliverer who would be born to the Genesis 3-predicted virgin in the future (before A.D. 70, as it turned out).
- Ahaz is told someone (Assyria, as it turned out) would within a few years dethrone the two kingdoms currently plotting against Israel.

Joseph plays a significant and underappreciated role in that first Isaiah promise. To see how, let's discuss the background on Messiah's family lines.

BACKGROUND ON MESSIAH'S FAMILY LINES

The New Testament begins with Matthew's genealogy of Messiah Jesus. Turning to Matthew 1, let's read the bookends of that genealogy.

> An account of the genealogy of Jesus Christ, the Son of David,
> the Son of Abraham:....
> and Jacob fathered Joseph the husband of Mary,
> who gave birth to Jesus who is called the Christ. (Matthew 1:1, 16)

In contemporary society, genetics and genealogy are big businesses. The main DNA-testing companies have handled millions of requests from people paying to determine their ethnic composition. Some of this interest is peaked by curiosity. Another motive concerns health issues, since determining genetic tendencies can assist with prophylactic treatment. All of those purposes are fine, but we should understand that they were not the reason classical Jews kept such careful genealogical records. They were and are concerned with something much bigger—the specific promises made by God about the future of Israel and the Messiah.

It's clear that Matthew 1 traces Joseph's family tree. But there is a vital subtlety that isn't evident in English. The first "who" in verse 16 is feminine in the Greek text. That is purposeful and telling. In fact, it shouts for attention, because the masculine form would have been used if Mary *and* Joseph were the parents. The text purposefully records "who" in the feminine only. Why? The only reasonable explanation is that only Mary was the biological parent of Jesus.

This matters greatly because Joseph's wing of the Davidic line was under a curse. The curse comes from Jeconiah. He was one of Joseph's forefathers, as Matthew points out "After the exile to Babylon Jeconiah fathered Shealtiel…" (Matthew 1:12) And all those descended from Jeconiah were under this specific curse God laid out through Jeremiah:

> This is what the Lord says:
> None of his descendants will succeed
> in sitting on the throne of David
> or ruling again in Judah. (Jeremiah 22:30)

There were many branches that came from David. Joseph's particular branch could not produce Messiah from Jeconiah's cursed seed.

Meanwhile, Luke relates the genealogy of Jesus from Mary's line, stating that "As he began his ministry, Jesus was about thirty years old and was *thought to be* the son of Joseph, son of Heli, son of Matthat, son of Levi, son of Melchi, son of Jannai…" (Luke 3:23–24)

This is another instance where English, for all its glories, has a difficult time doing justice to the original Koine Greek. Is it proper in English to say, "son of '*the*' Joseph, son of '*the*' Heli," and so on? Of course not! But it was exactly proper in Greek. In the Greek texts, there is a "*the*" in front of each name in Luke's genealogy. Each name, that is, except for one.

No "*the*" exists before Joseph! The lack of a "*the*" would have been a clear tip off to any classical reader that this is describing the line of his wife, not of Joseph. That's why the English translators supply "thought to be." What difference does it make? These genealogies disclose two significant points:

- Jesus is the legitimate heir of David outside the curse.
- Jesus is the legitimate son of God as He had no human father.

BACKGROUND ON MESSIAH'S CHARACTER

There is one last bit of necessary context to view for us to fully appreciate how the heavens put on a display, the constellations danced, and God changed the cold clay of earth. Matthew and Luke use very specific terms to reveal this:

> An account of the genealogy of Jesus Christ, the Son of David, the Son of Abraham… (Matthew 1:1)
>
> …son of Adam, son of God. (Luke 3:38)

Matthew's "Son of David" means Messiah is King. Christ, the Greek form of *Messiah,* declares that Jesus is the fulfillment of Isaiah. He is the King! Matthew then uses the term "Son of Abraham." That means Jesus is a Jew in the covenant of grace. To be a son of Abraham is different than being a Jew under Moses' law. The Abrahamic Covenant goes on forever. It is unilateral, a covenant of grace relying only on God. Thus, Jesus is not merely a Jew—related to Abraham through Isaac. He is part of the covenant of God's grace. Further, Matthew takes pains to show that Jesus fulfills the Mosaic Covenant and brings all who trust Him, Jew and Gentile, into that Abrahamic Covenant. One can visualize the argument from Matthew's Gospel in a simple diagram:

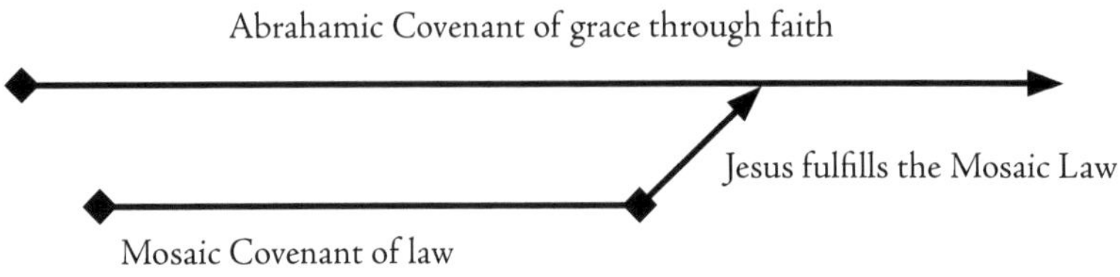

"Son of Adam" is the first phrase in Luke 3:38. It declares Yeshua is human. This Jesus is fully man, very human. The very next phrase juxtaposed on the son of Adam is "son of God." He is God. This child over whom Joseph is given responsibility is the Jewish God-Man King of grace.

JOSEPH'S RESPONSE

How does Joseph handle all the weight of this background, prophecy, and character? His response amazes and blesses us!

Matthew 1:20–24 contains the first part of his response:

> But after he had considered these things, an angel of the Lord appeared to him in a dream, saying, "Joseph, son of David, don't be afraid to take Mary as your wife, because what has been conceived in her is from the Holy Spirit. She will give birth to a son, and you are to name him Jesus, because he will save his people from their sins."
>
> Now all this took place to fulfill what was spoken by the Lord through the prophet:
>
> *See, the virgin will become pregnant*
> *and give birth to a son,*
> *and they will name him Immanuel,*
> which is translated "God is with us."

> When Joseph woke up, he did as the Lord's angel had commanded him. He married her but did not have sexual relations with her until she gave birth to a son. And he named him Jesus.

Verse 20 is so full of content! And the angel's statement is so much richer in light of the background. Joseph is indeed a son of David. But he knows that he is not the focus. His line is cut off. Yet that doesn't keep him from being a great father. Joseph is expected to name the boy. That means he assumes full parental responsibility because in that culture the granting of a name represented responsibility for guiding the one named.

Not much has changed in that respect. Did you ever receive a nickname from a teacher or coach whom you really respected? It speaks to a powerful kind of kinship. When the adult leader nicknames you, you know you belong. Horribly, the opposite happens with bullies. They give wicked nicknames in an effort to show their control by exclusion.

Joseph, son of David, is not a bully. He gives the greatest name of all to Immanuel. And in calling him Jesus, Joseph is reminded that salvation won't come through his blood. It will only come through his stepson's. Joseph accepted that. He obeyed. These verses indicate that everything in his life appears to point to Messiah. Joseph willingly surrenders for Jesus. That's what matters. That's what will change other lives. Poet Mary-Patrice Woehling captures Joseph's response and attitudes nicely in her poem "Joseph." She writes in one stanza:

> While Joseph worked and watched as Mary lay
> And nursed the baby. Sheep and oxen saw
> He scrubbed the trough and filled it with fresh hay;
> The constellations danced above cold clay.

Will we be like Joseph? Will we continually decrease so that Jesus might increase? Is that our focus? Will we work hard for Jesus to help dancing heaven change cold earth? What say you, Christian? Actually, we should ask, "Will we be like Jesus?" In a beautiful situational irony, Joseph's surrender is actually an imitation of his earthly son.

Our friend David Wade serves on a team that helped us prepare this study of Joseph. In a striking note, David explains how Joseph's self-surrender actually imitates the child for whom he cares:

> Joseph imitates Jesus. Philippians 2:7 describes Jesus as the One who "made himself nothing, taking the very nature of a servant." Wow, this is hard for us humans to do! Like Jesus, who surrendered glory for a trough, Joseph was all about serving God out of faith with "nothing in it for me." May we all be that way.[23]

About 100 years ago a young mother in West London named Kate Wilkinson was reading that same passage in Philippians 2. The poem and lyrics she wrote in response serve as a powerful summary of Joseph's focus and surrender:

> May the mind of Christ my Savior
> Live in me from day to day,
> By His love and power controlling
> All I do and say.
>
> May the Word of God dwell richly
> In my heart from hour to hour,
> So that all may see I triumph
> Only through His power.

May the peace of God my Father
Rule my life in everything,
That I may be calm to comfort
Sick and sorrowing.

May the love of Jesus fill me
As the waters fill the sea;
Him exalting, self abasing,
This is victory.

May I run the race before me,
Strong and brave to face the foe,
Looking only unto Jesus
As I onward go.[24]

Joseph willingly surrenders to the mind of Christ. Mark 6:1–3 contains Joseph's second response: He takes responsibility, a commitment he displays in apprenticing his stepson:

> He [Jesus the adult] left there and came to his hometown, and his disciples followed him. When the Sabbath came, he began to teach in the synagogue, and many who heard him were astonished. "Where did this man get these things?" they said. "What is this wisdom that has been given to him, and how are these miracles performed by his hands? Isn't this the carpenter, the son of Mary, and the brother of James, Joses, Judas, and Simon? And aren't his sisters here with us?" So they were offended by him.

The English word "carpenter" in verse 3 is a translation of *tekton,* (τέκτων) a general word for a builder. *Tektons* worked in stone as well as wood. Since there was very little wood for building in Israel, most *tekton* work was stone masonry. For example, it is almost certain that Joseph and Jesus—like every *tekton* nearby—worked stone for this boom town known as Scythopolis.

Jesus must have entered apprenticeship at 13; otherwise He would not be called *tekton*. That may explain part of the communal shock over His knowledge and wisdom. The people were especially astonished since Jesus never followed a teacher in higher education!

Scythopolis
(Photo by Janna Braudrick)

Earlier, we covered the normal flow of schooling for post-exile Jews. Here's a brief reminder of the practice among these first people to ever practice compulsory public education:

- Somewhere from 5–7 years, every child entered synagogue school.
- When a student turned 10, he or she could enter the *bet midrash*, secondary school, where older students and some adults studied Torah and rabbinic traditions.
- At 12 or 13, a student was considered subject to the commandments—the age of accountability for what they had been learning.

- At that point, most went to work or returned to the home and only attended school on occasion.

That must have been Jesus' path. Again, He would never be called *tekton* otherwise. That's significant, as it means He never got to join the pinnacle of education. The top education began at 13, when a few truly outstanding students left home and studied with a famous rabbi, but Jesus never got to go to "rabbi college." The white-collar snobs in Nazareth are dumbfounded. How could he know what He knows? Jesus' lack of schooling offended them! Even though they know him, they choose to be insulted over His refusal to fit their mold. They knew who He really was, and yet were still offended!

His lineage must have been understood, because in their comments Jesus is oddly called "the son of Mary." Normal usage would have been to call Jesus the son of Joseph—even if Joseph was by this time dead. The only explanation for saying "son of Mary" is that Jesus' true background was recognized. How damning! These people knew exactly who Jesus was—their own words convicted them. But they were determined to relegate Jesus into a comfortable, safe category they could control. In fact, they got so affronted they tried to stone Jesus by throwing him off this cliff outside their village (pictured on the next page).

This brings up a remarkable difference between Joseph and the religious leaders:

- Joseph accepted responsibility and surrendered control.
- The Nazareth synagogue leaders rejected responsibility and exerted control.

Wayne teaching at the Nazareth cliff
(Photo by Matt Lantz)

Thank goodness we are never like the people of Nazareth! We are always like Joseph. We always focus on Jesus, surrendering personal control as we accept responsibility to do right. We never get frustrated about losing control or avoid responsibility for acting on what we know...do we? Dear brethren, please, let's learn to surrender control to Jesus and accept responsibility to act in His name.

We know from the Bible that Joseph and Mary had at least six other children who survived into adulthood. We don't know what Joseph taught the others, though the scant evidence suggests he was a good father. But with Jesus, we know that Joseph responsibly taught the boy. He apprenticed him. That's why Jesus is called *tekton*.

What must it have been like to train a son like that? Joseph had to shepherd the God-Man-King! Musician Michael Card captured some of the likely difficulties in his lyrics "Joseph's Song:"

How could it be this baby in my arms
Sleeping now, so peacefully
The Son of God, the angel said
How could it be
Lord I know He's not my own
Not of my flesh, not of my bone
Still Father let this baby be
The son of my love
Father show me where I fit into this plan of yours
How can a man be father to the Son of God
Lord for all my life I've been a simple carpenter
How can I raise a king, How can I raise a king?[25]

Beautiful! Another member of our worship team, Brian Behrman, sent us a powerful note about these words and what they convey:

> There were many nights I was holding one of our babies, listening to Michael Card's "Joseph's Song" while I was trying to calm them down and get them to go to sleep for the night. As I looked at them, this overwhelming feeling would come over me: "God has chosen ME to be the dad to this child." That song has a line that Joseph probably prayed, and I certainly have: "Father show me where I fit into this plan of yours." I have never stopped praying that concerning my kids. My desire is to fulfill God's plan as an example to them and others of the character of Christ. I fall short in many ways, but such is my aim. Thanks for teaching on Joseph, who inspires us in that desire.[26]

Joseph shows exactly such character. He surrenders his rights in order to focus on Jesus. He responsibly apprentices his stepson.

And Joseph takes his son to worship in community. We see the evidence in Luke 2:41–50:

> Every year his parents traveled to Jerusalem for the Passover Festival. When he was twelve years old, they went up according to the custom of the festival. After those days were over, as they were returning, the boy Jesus stayed behind in Jerusalem, but his parents did not know it. Assuming he was in the traveling party, they went a day's journey. Then they began looking for him among their relatives and friends. When they did not find him, they returned to Jerusalem to search for him.
>
> After three days, they found him in the temple sitting among the teachers, listening to them and asking them questions. And all those who heard him were astounded at his understanding and his answers.
>
> When his parents saw him, they were astonished, and his mother said to him, "Son, why have you treated us like this? Your father and I have been anxiously searching for you."
>
> "Why were you searching for me?" he asked them. "Didn't you know that it was necessary for me to be in my Father's house?" But they did not understand what he said to them.

There are many fascinating things to learn here, but for this study let's again concentrate on the bookends of the passage. Verses 41 and 49 have a contrast that encapsulates Joseph's calling. Joseph is not Jesus' true Father (v. 49) yet he is fully Jesus' earthly parent (v. 41).

Like any committed Jewish father of the era, Joseph takes his family to Jerusalem every year for Passover. That was a three-day journey from Nazareth. It required just a bit more effort than most of us expended getting to church last Sunday. Maybe the effort required explains why many Jews made excuses not to go. Many young men didn't have the blessing of a parent like Joseph who would take them to communal worship.

There is a strong parallel to our time. Though we aren't under the now-fulfilled Mosaic Law to travel annually to Jerusalem, we are told in Hebrews 10:

> Let us hold on to the confession of our hope without wavering, since he who promised is faithful. And let us watch out for one another to provoke love and good works, not neglecting to gather together, as some are in the habit of doing, but encouraging each other, and all the more as you see the day approaching. (Hebrews 10:23–25)

We don't commit to the rhythm of group worship just for ourselves! We aren't *consumers* leaving reviews. We are a redeemed *community*. Look at the other-focus in the Hebrew 10 commands! "Us; our; gather together; one another; each other." That is a calling to be like Joseph, who did whatever it took—losing income, paying money to travel—all so he could shepherd his family in the invaluable practice of community worship.

Erica Komisar is a Jewish writer. Wayne has enjoyed finding some wisdom in her books, and was especially struck by these comments she made in a recent column:

> In an individualistic, narcissistic and lonely society, religion provides children a rare opportunity for natural community. The idea that hundreds of people can gather together and sing joyful prayers as a collective is a buffer against the emptiness of modern culture. It's more necessary than ever in a world where teens can have hundreds of virtual friends and few real ones,

> where parents are often too distracted physically or emotionally to soothe their children's distress. Today the U.S. is a competitive, scary and stressful place that idealizes perfectionism, materialism, selfishness and virtual rather than real human connection. Religion is the best bulwark against that kind of society. Spiritual belief and practice reinforce collective kindness, empathy, gratitude and real connection. Whether children choose to continue to practice as adults is something parents cannot control. But that spiritual or religious center will benefit them their entire lives.[27]

Two thousand years later, someone has finally caught up to Joseph! Joseph's response to God's invasion of his life includes three big takeaways:

- Joseph finds fulfillment in serving the Son of God. His all points to Messiah. Put poetically in the words of Mary-Patrice Woehling, he "scrubbed the trough" for Jesus.
- Joseph shows us how to invest in children, to shepherd and train them. Our missionary friend Dan Bolin summarizes well: "Whether you are a father or not, strive to mirror the life of Joseph. Obey God, serve faithfully, and help protect and direct the next generation." [28]
- Joseph emphasizes worship in community.

WHAT IS OUR LEGACY?

Now, bring this home to the present and yourself. Think about your family, especially during the Christmas holidays. While Christmas is often a time of family togetherness, it brings heavy stresses. Most families frantically make lists, purchase and wrap gifts, and meet together for reunions. On Christmas Eve or Christmas Day, the family unwraps and flings paper everywhere. Everyone eventually falls into a sugar coma on the floor and couches. After a few seconds of stillness, perhaps the thought slowly creeps into the Christian's mind, "What are we doing here? This stuff is fine, and it can express love, but what are we emphasizing? Is this really the meaning of Christmas?"

By contrast, we can be like Joseph. Presents and parties are great! We shouldn't avoid them, but rather enjoy everything as part of a life pointing to Messiah. We find fulfillment in serving the Son of God. It comes through in what we say and do. It flows out of us in giving and caring for others.

We invest properly in children. That may mean sacrificing for them. It almost surely doesn't mean giving them whatever they want. It means discipline as required. It means loving, guiding, and encouraging them.

We emphasize worship in community. We bring our extended family to the Christmas celebrations. And we don't give up meeting together as redeemed community.

4

LEAVE A POSITIVE IMPRESSION

JOSEPH LEFT AN IMPRESSION.

We should point out one more detail in Vincenzo de' Rossi's statue from the Roman Pantheon. Look at the hand on Jesus' shoulder. It is firm, guiding. De' Rossi captured the hand of a *tekton*—the Greek word for stonemason or carpenter we studied above.

Yet the touch is gentle. The child is smiling, not wincing. Joseph's attitude is strength at rest. Notice the set of the fingers and thumb. De' Rossi was a genius here: the digits are *cocked*! The fingers are slightly pushing from the hand through the fingertips. To grasp (no pun intended) the power of this, let's conduct a quick experiment. Place your hand on your thigh. Rest it flat, without pushing down. There is very little impression made in the fabric.

Now, rotate your wrist forward so the fingers are cocked, and the tips only are touching the fabric. What happens? Without increasing the pressure, there is an impression made. The fabric gives a little. It has an imprint from your fingers. De' Rossi is showing us something very important. Without being overbearing, Joseph left an impression on Jesus. You see Joseph's impact in the boy's face. There's a quiet confidence in the boy's countenance as he looks up from the Scripture and turns to face the world.

Through our investigation into Joseph, we've learned that Joseph was a major force in developing young Jesus. There is one big idea repeatedly shown to us in the Gospel texts—Joseph obeyed. In a manner rarely seen even among people who love and trust God, Joseph did exactly what God said. And he did so *every* time. As we learned in the last chapter, Joseph expressed that obedience through three means with respect to Jesus:

- He surrendered his rights.
- He taught Jesus to work.
- He emphasized worship.

That's how Joseph made an impactful impression. By the way, New Testament Greek has a marvelous word for that kind of dynamic impact. The term is τύπος transliterated as *tupos*. God has the Apostle Paul use *tupos* in reference to the Christians in Thessalonica, writing:

> And you became imitators of us and of the Lord, for you received the word in much affliction, with the joy of the Holy Spirit, so that you became an *example* to all the believers in Macedonia and Achaia. (1 Thessalonians 1:6–7 ESV)

The word we render "example" is *tupos*. Paul is saying a great deal by using that term. *Tupos* originally meant the mark left by a blow. For example, the 5th-century B.C. historian Herodotus used *tupos* to describe the black eye left after a fight. Over the next few hundred years, *tupos* came to mean a figure or pattern left imprinted in something—like the impression left in wax by a signet. That shift led to *tupos* being used almost always in a positive sense. Finally, by Paul's day, *tupos* came to signify any powerful impact, any impression indelibly left on somebody.

Now, let's think this through, as God intends. To leave a mark, you must be marked yourself. *Tupos* only occurs when something molded leaves an impression of its own shape. A classical signet can't leave an impression in wax until the signet is itself carved for the purpose. As a modern example, one Christmas Wayne's Dad gave him an embosser for books. It is shaped to leave an impression on the page of a book that says, "The library of Wayne Braudrick."

That is *tupos!* Joseph has been shaped by God, molded so that he leaves an impression.

JESUS WILLINGLY SUBMITS.

In an incredible passage, the end of Luke 2 shows how deep the impression was. Jesus continued each of Joseph's traits. Setting aside the real but incomprehensible issues raised by Jesus' deity, it is clear that Joseph left a very positive impression.

> Then he [Jesus] went down with them and came to Nazareth and was obedient to them. His mother kept all these things in her heart. (Luke 2:51])

Joseph obeyed, and Jesus does the same. Jesus willingly submits to His parents. By the way, the immediate context makes this even more impressive. The action just before this statement reveals how very easily Jesus could have justified *disobeying* them. We read the passage below earlier, but it is worth a second reading to emphasize this point:

> Every year his parents traveled to Jerusalem for the Passover Festival. When he was twelve years old, they went up according to the custom of the festival. After those days were over, as they were returning, the boy Jesus stayed behind in Jerusalem, but his parents did not know it. Assuming he was in the traveling party, they went a day's journey. Then they began looking for him among their relatives and friends. When they did not find him, they returned to Jerusalem to search for him.
>
> After three days, they found him in the temple sitting among the teachers, listening to them and asking them questions. And all those who heard him were astounded at his understanding and his answers.
>
> When his parents saw him, they were astonished, and his mother said to him, "Son, why have you treated us like this? Your father and I have been anxiously searching for you."
>
> "Why were you searching for me?" he asked them. "Didn't you know that it was necessary for me to be in my Father's house?" But they did not understand what he said to them. (Luke 2:41–50)

They didn't understand! How many pre-teens (and teens) have said that to a parent? "You just don't get it, Dad!" "Mom, you don't understand!" Unlike our parents—who in reality probably read our situations quite clearly—Jesus' parental units really *didn't* understand. Remember, Jesus was trained by God the Father privately. Fully human, Jesus was blessed to receive special training directly from God the Father. In the beautiful words of Isaiah 50:4, "morning by morning" the Father roused His Son for personal discipleship.

Jesus is the God-Man: one person with two distinct natures. Though omniscient as God, Jesus still needed to be instructed like every human. He received a double dose, learning via the Jewish education system and the greatest Private Tutor ever. The Father's schooling was so complete that 12-year-old Jesus was able to understand the Scriptures and explain them in a manner that amazed the doctors of law in the Temple district of Jerusalem. One of our favorite representations is the 1662 painting *Jesus Christ at Age Twelve* by the Dutch artist and student of Remabrant, Gerbrand van den Eeckhout.

Jesus Christ at Age Twelve
(Public domain)

This human boy is God the Son. He is taught every day directly by God the Father. He turns the Jerusalem Temple upside down as he spends about five days engaging the scriptural experts and amazing them with His knowledge. [29] Yet He was *still* obedient to His human parents. Look again at Luke 2:51. Jesus went with them and was obedient to them. That is absolutely amazing! Consider what that means:

- First, this proves that submission has nothing to do with inferiority. When Scripture calls for obedience or submission, it's become almost a reflex action for contemporary readers or listeners to stiffen. Why? Because we think that being subject to someone means you are inferior to them. That is incorrect and disproven by millennia of human experience. It is also disproven by Jesus. Jesus is certainly not inferior to Joseph and Mary. He's God the Son! He's Immanuel, God with us. Yet he obeys them. He had every right to resist, but he surrendered that right and chose to obey them.
- Second, Luke 2:51 shows that Jesus obeys in a manner similar to Joseph. Joseph understood little of what God was commanding, but he obeyed the Heavenly Father anyway. Jesus understood much more than any human, but he obeyed human parents anyway.

In fact, Jesus' obedience is predicted in the rest of that Isaiah passage:

> The Lord God has opened my ear,
> and I was not rebellious;
> I turned not backward.

> I gave my back to those who strike,
> and my cheeks to those who pull out the beard;
> I hid not my face
> from disgrace and spitting.
> But the Lord God helps me;
> therefore I have not been disgraced;
> therefore I have set my face like a flint,
> and I know that I shall not be put to shame. (Isaiah 50:5–7)[30]

Here Jesus submits to the *Heavenly* Father. He obeys His mission parameters, despite the personal pain.

As followers of Jesus, we should take note and consider our life mission. If we are going to see it fulfilled, we must set ourselves to obey, no matter what. Writing a nice vision statement on the wall achieves almost nothing. That's true in your church, your company, and your home. Goals and values are great! Mission and vision are important. But they all accomplish nothing without committed submission. In fact, without obedience empowered by God, missions, goals, and values become translucent dead weights that drag on an organization, church, or family.

Without obedience, mission cannot be fulfilled. With obedience, there is growth. That's why Luke brilliantly follows chapter 2 verse 51, covering Jesus' submission, with verse 52, detailing His growth:

> Then he went down with them and came to Nazareth and was obedient to them. His mother kept all these things in her heart.
>
> And Jesus increased in wisdom and stature, and in favor with God and with people.

JESUS GROWS IN WISDOM.

Jesus increases, first of all in wisdom. In fact, this is the second mention of Jesus' wisdom in Luke, the first coming when he was a little boy! Luke 2:40 reads, "And the child (παιδίον, transliterated as *paidion* = young or tender-aged child) grew and became strong, filled with wisdom. And the favor of God was upon him."[31]

Jesus grew in wisdom. We have spent some time thinking about this, trying to distill growth in wisdom into tidy transferable concepts. Here are our conclusions: humility, embracing a challenge, and personal responsibility are the three foundations of wisdom. Everything leading to wisdom flows from these three traits: embracing challenge, taking personal responsibility, and being humble. For now, we only have space to spend on the most important one—humility.

To grow in wisdom, *humility* is required. The entire book of Proverbs is dedicated to engendering wisdom, and it begins with humility:

> The proverbs of Solomon son of David, king of Israel:
> For learning wisdom and discipline;
> for understanding insightful sayings;
> for receiving prudent instruction
> in righteousness, justice, and integrity;
> for teaching shrewdness to the inexperienced,
> knowledge and discretion to a young man… (Proverbs 1:1–4)

Solomon begins with four "fors." See that? The tension builds as he sets up the big idea. It's like a full orchestral Beethoven crescendo rising, "for…for…for…for…" For wisdom and all its attendant blessings…

let a wise person listen and increase learning,
and let a discerning person obtain guidance (Proverbs 1:5)

Listen. Learn. Ask for guidance. Get help. There is an obvious and implied humility required for that. Only when we are humble will we learn, ask, and listen. And Solomon increases the punch by saying that this applies to those who are *already* wise and discerning! We must never stop growing.

Yet since the Garden of Eden, humans have struggled with humility. The great English poet John Milton, the author of *Paradise Lost,* was probably right in saying that pride is humanity's besetting sin. Our age is particularly rough on anyone wanting to grow in wisdom. There is so little listening and learning today, in part, because humility is so rare.

For example, lack of humility appears to be a big reason that test scores in public education keep dropping—American students for generations have been told how smart they are already. Everyone passes and everyone gets a trophy. There are no wrong answers. The student is always right. Grace isn't needed because you are already perfect.

Compare that with the way Jesus was taught in synagogue school. Look again at the main rules for the incredibly successful Jewish system:

- The rabbi holds "kingship" over the school.
- Students stand until invited to sit.
- A student cannot leave without permission.
- All stand when the teacher enters or leaves.
- The teacher is only ever called "Rabbi."

- School meets seven days a week, except for harvest. On Shabbat, students review all learned during the week.

That is likely a better formula for humility—and thus wisdom—than our current mantra of "the student is always right." Of course, pride still flourished in the hearts of students in Galilee. Nonetheless, it was likely easier for them to learn because that kind of discipline can help prepare one for the humility necessary to grow in wisdom. Just meditate on this astonishing, humbling truth: Jesus, who is God the Son and who was taught by God the Father every morning, stood up to honor a merely *human* rabbi! That's incredible humility! And it caused Jesus, who is also fully human, to grow in wisdom.

Jesus is living proof that humility isn't thinking less of oneself. *Humility is thinking of self properly while thinking primarily of others.*

Solomon isn't done with his thesis. He repeats the formula in verses 6–7; this time zeroing in on the most important source of wisdom—God.

> ...for understanding a proverb or a parable,
> the words of the wise, and their riddles.
> The fear of the Lord
> is the beginning of knowledge;
> fools despise wisdom and discipline. (Proverbs 1:6–7)

Humility is required if one is going to become wiser. It bears repeating that humility isn't thinking less of oneself, but rather thinking of self properly while thinking primarily of others. And that proper understanding of self can only come from God. It is in relationship to Him that we understand who we really are. God shows that we are:

- Made in His image
- Fallen/sinful as that image has been defaced
- Loved by Him
- Rescued by God's grace alone through faith alone

Rumination on those scriptural truths fosters humility. We recognize our worth and our wretchedness. We grasp our absolute inability to save ourselves and the wonderful truth that God has made a way for our salvation.

JESUS GROWS IN STATURE

Jesus grew in wisdom and He developed in stature. That means He developed physically as well as intellectually and spiritually. Wayne once asked a respected Christian philosopher why the resurrection of the body is so important in Scripture. Getting new bodies after sin is eliminated seemed unimportant to Wayne. The great thing will be eternity in God's presence. The physicality of the form seemed superfluous.

But that scholar's pithy response changed Wayne's thinking. The professor very simply said, "God likes bodies." God likes bodies. He created them for humans. He made the most intricate machine possible, and even after humans let sin ruin them, God still likes bodies. In fact, He chose to dwell in a body as God the Son. Further, God chooses to indwell humans, somehow incorporating our physical bodies as part of the Holy Spirit's dwelling. The Apostle Paul's synopsis is inspirational:

> Don't you [Christians] know that your body
> is a temple of the Holy Spirit who is in you,
> whom you have from God?
> You are not your own, for you were bought at a price.
> So glorify God with your body. (1 Corinthians 6:19–20)

God cares about bodies. So much so that by His Spirit, humans can glorify God with physical bodies! Further, the life described for Christians in eternity is a very physical one. The curse will be undone. Bodies, like souls, will be perfect and we will use them forever.

With all that in mind, consider how important it is that Jesus grows strong in stature. Jesus took care of His body—an amazing fact given that He knew He would have a perfect resurrection form in just a few years. If there was ever a teen who could have been excused for abusing his body, it was Jesus. Yet instead of misusing his physical frame, Jesus grew in stature.

Please don't misunderstand. Jesus didn't worship his body or overdevelop it. As Isaiah foretold, "He had no stately form or physical majesty" (Isaiah 53:2). Neither do most of us! In fact, we have many infirmities of varying severity. But that doesn't matter. We can still take care of whatever body God has given us.

In 2019, a viral video revealed two Corgi dogs in Szechuan, China. They were "working out" on side-by-side treadmills. The dog on the left is looking ahead, pumping his little legs, doing hard work to keep his stature as strong as is possible for a Corgi. The right one is looking for attention and pretending to care for his body. He has one paw occasionally touching the moving tread while he looks up at the people around for approval. Fellow doggies, which Corgi best resembles you? Let's be like the Corgi on the left! Let's reasonably care for our bodies.

Remember, Joseph taught Jesus by three great examples:

- He surrendered his rights.
- He taught Jesus to work.
- He emphasized worship.

The second one. work, requires the very things mentioned in Luke 2:52. If we stagnate in knowledge, the marketplace passes by us. We must keep growing in skill. We must take care of our bodies for as long as God intends for us to have them. Jesus was a *tekton,* for goodness' sake! In Israel, He would have worked most of the time in stone. You can't last as a stonemason if you don't watch out for your body. Jesus grew in wisdom and stature.

JESUS GROWS IN FAVOR WITH PEOPLE.

One other thing is necessary for healthy work—being likable. Favor with people is especially important for a small businessman like a *tekton*. If you're a jerk, business dies out. Luke says that they *favored* Him. People liked Jesus.

His attitude may explain why. Jesus was a servant. He led by serving people. From His surrender of heaven...to taking the form of humanity...to being subject to His parents...to washing feet... to willingly dying on the cross...Jesus *descended* into greatness.

A young man in Arkansas forwarded a great example of this to us. Brothers Aaron and Jesse Stone lead a rock band called My Epic, and their song "Lower Still" captures Jesus' descent into greatness:

look, he's covered in dirt
the blood of his mother has mixed with the earth
and she's just a child who's throbbing in pain
from the terror of birth by the light of a cave

now they've laid that small baby
where creatures come eat
like a meal for the swine who have no clue that he
is still holding together the world that they see
they don't know just how low he has to go
lower still

look now he's kneeling he's washing their feet
though they're all filthy fishermen, traitors and thieves
now he's pouring his heart out and they're falling asleep
but he has to go lower still

there is greater love to show
hands to the plow
further down now
blood must flow

all these steps are personal
all his shame is ransom
oh do you see, do you see just how low, he has come
do you see it now?
no one takes from him
what he freely gives away

beat in his face
tear the skin off his back
lower still, lower still
strip off his clothes

make him crawl through the streets
lower still, lower still
hang him like meat
on a criminal's tree

lower still, lower still
bury his corpse in the earth
like a seed, like a seed, like a seed
lower still, lower still

the earth explodes
she cannot hold him!
and all therein is placed beneath him
and death itself no longer reigns
it cannot keep the ones he gave himself to save
and as the universe shatters the darkness dissolves
he alone will be honored
we will bathe in his splendor
as all heads bow lower still
all heads bow lower still[32]

That's good! Want to have influence, to grow in favor with people? *Serve* them. Go lower still. Joseph taught that. He impressed surrender. He taught *tekton,* which requires wisdom, stature, and favor with people.

JESUS EMPHASIZES WORSHIP.

Joseph also taught Jesus to worship, as evidenced by the family commitment to both annual Temple journeys and local synagogue engagement. Thus, it's no surprise that Jesus emphasizes worship in His life and ministry.

Luke tells us that Jesus grew in favor with God. That is a necessity for any person to enjoy the relationship with the Heavenly Father. Of course, one may rightly wonder, "How could Jesus grow in favor with God when He is God?" Our friend Martin MacDonald offered this great answer:

> As fully man, Jesus experienced all of the things that mankind does. Thus He is qualified to be Savior and also able to relate to us and the struggles of life this side of heaven. His relationship with the Father described in Luke must be seen in this context.[33]

Think about all the time Jesus spent in the Temple, in prayer, in Scripture, in worshipping the Father. He learned all that from his earthly father, not merely the Heavenly Father. Joseph took Jesus to the annual Passover celebration, sacrificing to bring his family to communal worship. Such willing sacrifice is a huge factor in teaching children how to grow in favor with God.

You may have read that church attendance is falling rapidly in many Western countries. Besides being a spiritual tragedy in many lives, it leads to serious societal problems. However, the cause of this that you hear the most about is the church. Many commentators seem to think the only way to increase church engagement is to radically change churches.

But our research and experience suggests the attendance slide experienced in many places is not because of churches, though there is always much to change and improve about every local body of Christians. The one very clear cause of decline in worship attendance is a lack of healthy fathering! Think it through…

Why give Jesus a superfluous human stepfather? Joseph isn't necessary. Yet, for growing in favor with God, *fathering* makes all the difference. In his book *Whatever Happened to Manhood*, Wayne examined the very thorough studies on this conducted in Switzerland and the United States. Rather than retread that information, we will share a summary of those conclusions, coupled with two other studies conducted by Lifeway:

> The research on the impact of a dad's faith and practice on their families is [overwhelming]...if a father does not go to church, even if his wife does, only 1 child in 50 will become a regular worshiper. If a father does go regularly, regardless of what the mother does, between two-thirds and three-quarters of their children will attend church as adults. If a father attends church irregularly, between half and two-thirds of their kids will attend church with some regularity as adults.

Another study, focused on Sunday School, found similar results on the impact of fathers:

- When both parents attend Bible study in addition to the Sunday service, 72% of their children attend Sunday school when grown.
- When only the father attends Sunday school, 55% of the children attend when grown.
- When only the mother attends Sunday school, 15% of the children attend when grown.
- When neither parent attends Sunday school, only 6% of the children attend when grown.

> Another survey found that if a child is the first person in a household to become a Christian, there is a 3.5% probability everyone else in the household will follow. If the mother is the first to become a Christian, there is a 17% probability everyone else in the household will follow. However, when the father is first, there is a 93% probability everyone else in the household will follow.[34]

These observations do not denigrate the importance of mothers. However, if you want to increase worship, you need to increase the influence of good men. And therein lies the clear problem in Western countries. Fathers are absent. Therefore, children develop an anti-Joseph lifestyle. While Joseph willingly surrendered his rights to what was best for all, we today demand our supposed rights. Joseph taught work, but people now increasingly shirk labor. Joseph led his family to worship. Without that kind of leadership, a culture deemphasizes worship.

But what if there's no father in the life of children you love? Does the absence of a Joseph condemn those children to miss the blessings of discipleship? Perish the thought! In our practice, we have personally seen the following steps positively change the lives of the fatherless or spiritually fatherless:

- Thank God that He is and always will be Father to the fatherless. Every person can always engage with the Father who never leaves. (Psalm 68:5)
- Get into a church life group or class where those children can come to know godly men.
- In almost every local church, there are true gentlemen who serve children. Take advantage of the opportunities

> that offers. Get boys into ministries like Trail Life. Sign up children for ministries like AWANA. Bring children to Sunday school and youth. It makes a massive difference.

If you are one of those men blessed to influence young lives, be like Joseph. Emphasize worship. Whether you are working, reading, playing, walking, let all your life be worship to the Lord.

Jesus was blessed. His earthly father's business was to encourage the Heavenly Father's business. That's why the sculptor Vincenzo de Rossi has Jesus holding the scroll of Scripture in His hands as Joseph makes an impression. It's also what makes Luke 2:49 so brilliant: "it was necessary for me to be in my Father's house." That phrase "in my father's house" could be and often is translated "about my father's business."

Knowing Luke's love for subtle nuance, it's very likely Jesus speaks here about both his fathers. There is no capitalization of "Father" in the original texts, so Jesus may be pointing out that his earthly father's most important business is worship. That's the *tupos*—the impact—Joseph leaves. He impresses submission, growth, and worship.

OUR IMPRESSION

What kind of impression are you leaving? If our *tupos* is positive, the people we engage will submit to God's will, grow strong, and emphasize worship. But in order to pass that on we must first see those traits developed in ourselves.

Joseph and Jesus surrendered rights. That doesn't mean they didn't stand for right! Joseph fled oppression. Jesus cleansed the Temple. But overall, Joseph and Jesus taught that we are to be subjection to authorities, even those who appear much less advanced than are we. How well do you and I do at that? We hear a lot of words of indignancy, entitlement, and outrage these days. We hear much less about submission to God's will. That must change if we are to live like Joseph and Jesus lived. We also need to *work* at the things God has given us to do. And whatever those jobs are, we need to keep growing wiser, taking care of our bodies that God loves, and growing in favor by serving everyone. Above all, we need to grow in favor with God. Joseph emphasized worship and his stepson grew in favor with God. By His grace, may we do the same.

5
FOLLOW THE STAR

Throughout this study of Joseph, we have been gripped especially by Joseph's main trait. Joseph is faithful. That's why we titled the book *Faithful Father*.

Joseph is faithful. In fact, he is so full of faith that in every situation Joseph trusts God enough to obey exactly what God commands! That same idea is behind the origins of the English term "faithful." Our forebears created the word to describe a person full of faith, full of trust in God. Yet over a fairly brief period of time, the main *result* of being full of faith began to dominate the definition.

- Originally (early 14th c.): full of faith = one who trusts God.
- Developed as (late 14th c.): reliable = one who obeys; follows through.

The shift is fine, linguistically and theologically. However, one must remember that the first definition remains at the core of the latter one. It is only because of trust in God that a "faithful" person can be trustworthy, reliable, and obedient. And Joseph powerfully exemplifies that dynamic. With every command God gives, however large or unexpected, Joseph is faithful.

By God's grace, we also can be faithful. In fact, there are Joseph-like stories playing out all around us, if we will just stop and notice them.

For example, a few weeks ago, a young man at our church became a believer in Jesus. He was drawn to the Bible and, with some help and direction, began studying it. A couple of days later, this brand-new Christian placed money in the offering box. His friend observed the gift and asked him why he did that. Our new brother replied, "I read in the Bible that God says to give." That's faithfulness!

That same week, an older woman shared with us that she was struggling mightily with hating her neighbor. She just couldn't get over the loudness and lunacy of the people next door. But then she chose to trust God, to engage the Lord at a deeper level. She began to meditate on truths like Paul's command, "Be kind and compassionate to one another, forgiving one another, just as God also forgave you in Christ." (Ephesians 4:32)

When our friend began to look at her situation that way—acting out of her trust in Christ who forgave her own sins—then she was empowered to obey God. She now makes a conscious choice every day to love her neighbor. That is following the lead of the remarkable Joseph, where trust in God leads to trustworthiness.

As long as we are discussing difficult but important matters, here are a few questions sparked by our study of Joseph:

- Do I do what I am told when I am told it?

- Unless they are commanding me to disobey God, do I immediately obey the appropriate authorities in my life?
- Am I obeying God?
- Instead of doing right, am I manipulating, lying, or using shortcuts at work or home?
- Am I twisting God's commands so that I can get what I desire while pretending to obey God?

Such uncomfortable questions can cause people to squirm. We understand as we feel the same discomfort. But instead of fleeing that conviction, let's be still for a moment and reflect. What might be the source of our unsettled feelings? In our practice, we have noted that fear usually plays a big part. So does hurt.

In our pain and fear, Christians sometimes start following other things instead of God's Word. We stubbornly follow our own plans rather than seeking and following God's plans for us. Sometimes God's instructions don't seem sufficient or sensical to us. So, we reject them, usually with sidewinding motion comprised of rationalization dynamically paired with manipulation. Most believers in Jesus don't intend to become wayward or killjoys; but that crooked rationalization/manipulation motion becomes our norm, until we become confused about what really constitutes forward motion. Matthew Thiessen explains the situation perfectly in his lyrics to the song "Forward Motion":

> We all struggle with forward motion
> 'Cause forward motion is harder than it sounds
> Well every time I gain some ground
> I gotta turn myself around.[35]

It is precisely then, in the midst of our struggle with forward motion, that we need to see examples like Max the dog and Joseph the faithful father and modern people who do what's right. Those examples show us again how to obediently follow the right path. Pastor Max Lucado explained this really well in his book *In the Manger:*

> Joseph didn't let his confusion disrupt his obedience. He didn't know everything. But he did what he knew. He shut down his business, packed up his family, and went to another country. Why? Because that's what God said to do. What about you? Just like Joseph, you can't see the whole picture. Just like Joseph, your task is to see that Jesus is brought into your part of the world. And just like Joseph, you have a choice: to obey or disobey. Because Joseph obeyed, God used him to change the world.[36]

Friends, we should imitate the wise people of every age and follow the Christmas star. Not the shekinah glory the magi tracked, but the star Joseph. Joseph shines light on two big ideas:

- Christians need to obey, to be faithful. We need to trust God such that we obey His Word. No more excuses. First-time obedience.
- For those who have never believed in Jesus as Savior, Joseph clearly points to trust. You can't really obey until you trust. Our forebears understood that and built the idea right into the meaning of the word faithful!

There is one way to live like Joseph and the fate that is the human norm. Trust and obey. As the young man testified at Moody's meeting in Boston, "I don't understand everything. But I am going to trust. And I am going to obey." Let's get up and go do likewise.

ENDNOTES

1 William Barclay, *The Gospel of Matthew*, Volume 1, 32 Note: late in life, Dr. Barclay developed some heretical and unbiblical ideas. He can be very helpful, but please read with discernment.

2 Unless otherwise noted, all verses taken from the Christian Standard Bible (CSB).

3 Photo by Jared Coe, used with permission.

4 Arnold Fruchtenbaum, *Yeshua: The Life of the Messiah from a Messianic Jewish Perspective*, Vol. 1, 338–39.

5 Raymond Brown, *The Birth of the Messiah*, 124.

6 Cicero, *The Speech of Cicero in Defense of Cluentius* (1895), 32.

7 Sefaria.org *Mishnah Kethuboth 1:5; TalBab Kethuboth 9b, 12a;* retrieved August 20, 2021.

8 Fruchtenbaum, *Yeshua*, Vol 1, 340 (italics not in original).

9 Samuel Lachs, *A Rabbinic Commentary of the New Testament: the Gospels of Matthew, Mark, and Luke*, 6.

10 Fruchtenbaum, *Yeshua* Vol. 1, 345.

11 Barclay, *The Gospel of Matthew*, 11.

12 Ibid, 16.

13 https://songscoops.blogspot.com/2018/09/trust-and-obey-john-h-sammis.html, retrieved August 19, 2021.

14 Donald D. Binder, *Into the Temple Courts: The Place of the Synagogues in the Second Temple Period,* 204–26. See also Lee I. Levine, *The Ancient Synagogue: The First Thousand Years,* 2nd ed., 50, 142–43.

15 Alfred Edersheim, *Sketches of Jewish Social Life,* 100–101.

16 Fruchtenbaum, *Yeshua,* Vol. 1, 477–78.

17 https://en.wikipedia.org/wiki/Dem_Bones retrieved August 20, 2021.

18 Fruchtenbaum, *Yeshua,* Vol. 1, 414.

19 Soniclight.org *Thomas Constable's Notes on Matthew,* retrieved January 4, 2021.

20 Barclay, 30.

21 Mary-Patrice Woehling, "Joseph" *First Things* December 2019.

22 Fruchtenbaum *Yeshua,* Vol. 1, 393.

23 David Wade, private correspondence in author's collection.

24 Kate Wilkinson, "May The Mind of Christ My Savior." https://hymnstudiesblog.wordpress.com/2009/03/31/quot-may-the-mind-of-christ-my-saviorquot/ retrieved December 4, 2019.

25 Michael Card, "Joseph's Song."

26 Brian Behrman, private correspondence in author's collection.

27 Erica Komisar, "Don't Believe in God? Lie to Your Children," *Wall Street Journal* 5 December 2019.

28 Dan Bolin, *Refueling in Flight blog,* retrieved December 3, 2019.

29 While serving as scholar-in-residence on our church staff, Doug Greenwold made a compelling case for five days. In a letter to Wayne, he wrote: "We typically view this passage as Jesus spending three days in the Temple. Perhaps it was more likely five days. On the first day, Mary and Joseph walk 15 miles north from Jerusalem in the male-female segregated caravans used by orthodox Jews. Only at the end of that day do they realize Jesus is missing (2:42). That requires them to find another segregated caravan heading south to retrace yesterday's steps, likely consuming at least another day. Only after Joseph and Mary return to Jerusalem can they begin looking for Jesus. Luke tells us they spent three days searching for Him (2:46). That suggests Jesus might have been on His own for five days."

30 The English Standard Version.

31 Ibid.

32 Aaron and Jesse Stone, "Lower Still."

33 Martin MacDonald, private correspondence in author's collection.

34 Nick Cady, "The Impact on Kids of Dad's Faith and Church Attendance" nickcady.org, June 20, 2016, https://nickcady.org/?s=Impact+on+kids retrieved December 3, 2021.

35 Matthew Thiessen, "Forward Motion."

36 Max Lucado, *In the Manger*, 12.

BIBLIOGRAPHY

BOOKS

Barclay, William. *The Gospel of Matthew*, Vol. 1, rev. ed. Louisville, KY: Presbyterian Publishing Group, 2001.

Binder, Donald D. *Into the Temple Courts: The Place of the Synagogues in the Second Temple Period*. Atlanta, GA: Society of Biblical Literature, 1999.

Brown, Raymond .*The Birth of the Messiah*. New Haven, CT: Yale University Press, 1999.

Cicero, *The Speech of Cicero in Defense of Cluentius (1895)*. Whitefish, MT: Kessinger Publishing, 2010.

Edersheim, Alfred *Sketches of Jewish Social Life*. Peabody, MA: Hendrickson Publishing, 1994.

Fruchtenbaum, Arnold *Yeshua: The Life of the Messiah from a Messianic Jewish Perspective*, Vol. 1. San Antonio: Ariel Ministries, 2016.

Lachs, Samuel *A Rabbinic Commentary of the New Testament: the Gospels of Matthew, Mark, and Luke*. Brooklyn: KTAV Publishing, 1987.

Levine, Lee I. *The Ancient Synagogue: The First Thousand Years, 2nd ed.* New Haven: Yale University Press, 2005.

Lucado, Max *In the Manger*. Nashville: Thomas Nelson, 2014.

ARTICLES AND LETTERS

Behrman, Brian private correspondence in author's collection. Used with permission.

Cady, Nick "The Impact on Kids of Dad's Faith and Church Attendance" nickcady.org, June 20, 2016.

Greenwold, Doug private correspondence in author's collection. Used with permission.

Komisar, Erica "Don't Believe in God? Lie to Your Children" *Wall Street Journal* December 5, 2019.

MacDonald, Martin private correspondence in author's collection. Used with permission.

Wade, David private correspondence in author's collection. Used with permission.

Woehling, Mary-Patrice "Joseph," *First Things* December 3, 2019.

WEBSITES

Bolin, Dan *Refueling in Flight blog*

Sefaria.org *Mishnah Kethuboth* and *TalBab Kethuboth*

Soniclight.org *Thomas Constable's Notes on Matthew*

MUSIC

Card, Michael. *Joseph's Song*. Brentwood, TN: Sparrow Records, 1988.

Johnson, James. *Dem Bones*. New York: Decca, 1926.

Sammis, John. *Trust and Obey*. Public domain.

Stone, Aaron and Jesse. *Lower Still*. Fallbrook, CA: Facedown Records, 2019.

Thiessen, Matthew. *Forward Motion*. Franklin, TN: Goatee Records, 2003.

Wilkinson, Kate. *May The Mind of Christ My Savior*. Public domain.

ABOUT THE AUTHORS

Wayne Braudrick serves as Lead Pastor of Frisco Bible Church in Frisco, Texas. He also teaches through the All the Difference daily radio broadcast and podcast. Dr. Braudrick earned his doctorate in leadership communication through Middlesex University in London and earned a master's degree in Bible at Dallas Theological Seminary; and was a National Merit Scholar at Baylor University where he read history, literature, and education. Wayne lives with his marvelous family in Frisco, Texas.

Jeremy Mikeska serves as Executive Pastor of Spiritual Formation of Frisco Bible Church in Frisco, Texas. He is a graduate of Texas A&M University and has been on the staff of Frisco Bible Church since 2005. He is an avid musician and soccer and softball player (or was before the broken leg thing mentioned in the text ☺) and enthusiastic Texas Rangers fan. Jeremy and his wife Jenni have four children, Murphy, the part coon hound howls a lot, and two cats, Ryder and Lainie. Yep, it's a zoo!

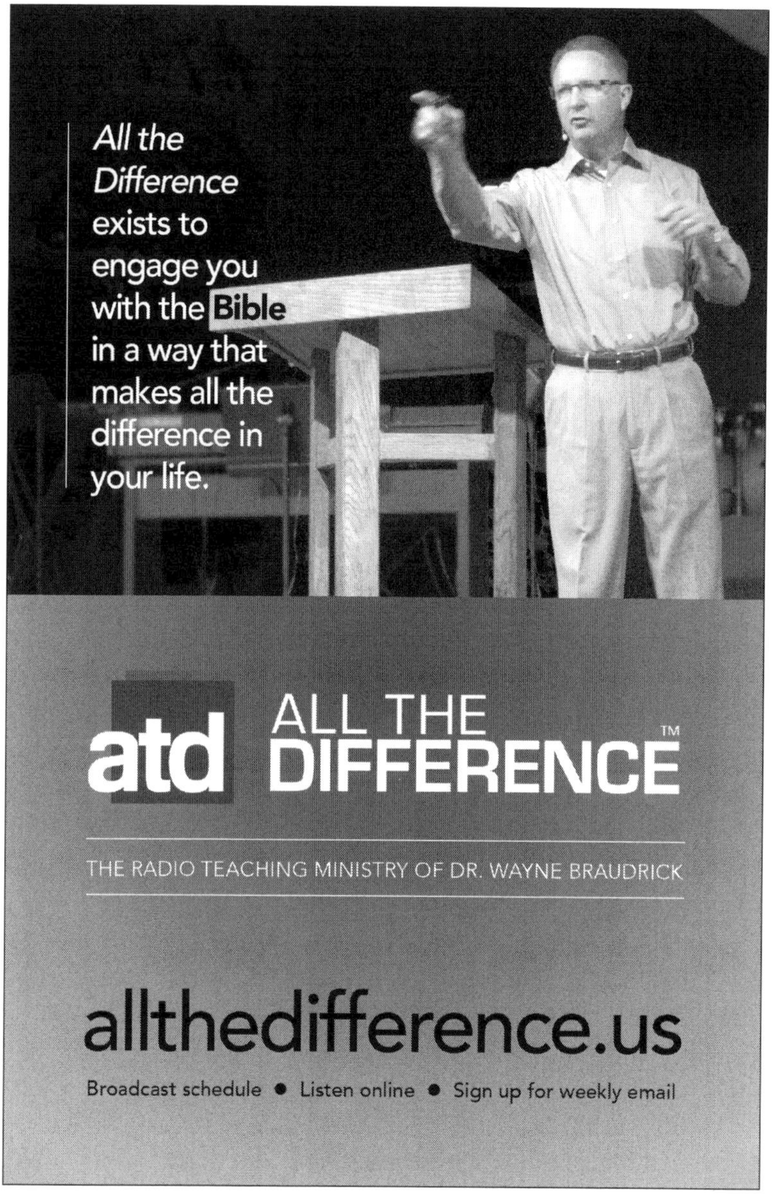

All the Difference exists to engage you with the Bible in a way that makes all the difference in your life.
atd
ALL THE DIFFERENCE™
THE RADIO TEACHING MINISTRY OF DR. WAYNE BRAUDRICK
allthedifference.us
Broadcast schedule • Listen online • Sign up for weekly email